Manual 30

Relating Consumer, Descriptive, and Laboratory Data to Better Understand Consumer Responses

Alejandra M. Muñoz, editor

ASTM Publication Code Number (PCN):
28-030097-36

ASTM
100 Barr Harbor Drive
West Conshohocken, PA 19428-2959

Printed in the U.S.A.

Library of Congress Cataloging-in-Publication Data

Relating consumer, descriptive, and laboratory data to better
understand consumer responses/Alejandra M. Muñoz, editor.
(Manual; 30); Includes bibliographical references and index.
ISBN 0-8031-2073-7
1. Commercial products—Testing. 2. Sensory evaluation.
3. Consumers—Research. I. Muñoz, Alejandra M., 1957–
II. Series: ASTM manual series ; MNL 30.
TX335.R435 1997
664′ .07—dc21 96-52055
CIP

Printed in Scranton, PA
February 1997

Foreword

This manual, *Relating Consumer, Descriptive, and Laboratory Data to Better Understand Consumer Responses,* was approved by Committee E-18 on Sensory-Evaluation of Materials and Products and developed by Task Group E.18.08.05. The editor was Alejandra M. Muñoz, Sensory Spectrum, Inc., 24 Washington Avenue, Chatham, NJ 07928.

Contents

Preface

This publication covers the techniques and applications of consumer data relationships and was developed by members of Task Group E.18.08.05, which is part of the ASTM Committee E-18 on Sensory Evaluation. The manual is intended for sensory and market research professionals responsible for consumer testing and the interpretation of consumer data.

This document illustrates how consumer data can be further explored and interpreted through data relationships, that is, how other relevant product (e.g., descriptive, instrumental data) or consumer information (e.g., demographic, employee consumer data) may be related to consumer test data to more fully understand and interpret consumer responses. The scope of the task group was to develop a practical document that discusses the importance, the requirements, the techniques, and the applications of relating consumer data to other product or consumer information.

Chapter 1 presents a discussion of the importance, the types, and the applications of consumer data relationships and presents an overview of the sensory projects in which data relationships are useful.

Chapter 2 describes the requirements needed to complete these projects, which are samples, sensory and analytical methodology, and data entry/analysis capabilities.

Chapter 3 covers issues related to the validity of data relationships, and Chapter 4 presents the statistical techniques used for data relationships.

The methodology described in the first four chapters is illustrated through various case studies in Chapters 5–8. These case studies present the most common and important projects/cases in which consumer data are analyzed, fully interpreted, and sometimes predicted through analytical/laboratory or other consumer information (e.g., descriptive/attribute, instrumental, consumer/market factors, and employee consumer data).

Special acknowledgment is given to B. Thomas Carr, who provided advice on the statistical methodology used in this manual, and to Morten Meilgaard for his review comments. An appreciation is extended to Judy Heylmun, Doris Aldridge, and Mary Jenkins for the data sets provided and used in some of the case studies.

Alejandra Muñoz
Sensory Spectrum,
Chatham, NJ; editor

by Alejandra M. Muñoz[1]

Chapter 1—Importance, Types, and Applications of Consumer Data Relationships

I. Introduction

Consumer research is one of the key activities of consumer products companies. Through this type of testing, companies determine consumer acceptance, preference, and opinions on the products tested. This is, ultimately, the most important type of information companies use to make product decisions, such as the development and marketing of new products, the reformulation of existing products, the acceptance of alternate suppliers and processes, the establishment of quality control specifications, etc.

The most common practice is to interpret and use the consumer information directly to answer research or marketing questions, such as:

1. Is there a difference in liking or preference between products?
2. Which product do consumers like or prefer?
3. What are the product characteristics consumers like and dislike?
4. How can a product be improved?

In the past few years, new and more complete data analysis techniques have been used in consumer research. It has been realized that, frequently, consumer data should not be interpreted and used by themselves, but should be studied in light of other product information to be fully understood.

The analysis of consumer data relationships is an approach that uses a variety of statistical techniques to relate consumer data to other information in order to gain a fuller understanding of consumer responses. The information most often related to consumer responses includes:

- descriptive analysis data (perceived sensory properties)
- instrumental/laboratory (physical or chemical data)
- company employee consumer data
- consumer and market factors (demographics)
- ingredient or process levels

In general, the benefits obtained from relating consumer data to the above information are:

- a more complete interpretation and understanding of consumer responses

[1]Technical director, Sensory Spectrum, Inc., 24 Washington Avenue, Chatham, NJ 07928.

- the potential ability to predict consumer responses using other information (e.g., descriptive, instrumental, employee consumer)

II. Types of Data Relationships

Table 1 shows several classifications of data relationships as viewed by this author. These classifications are not mutually exclusive, since a study can fall into several categories depending on its objectives and execution.

A. Sequential and Simultaneous Consumer Data Relationships

This classification is explained by Muñoz and Chambers [*1*]. Sequential and simultaneous consumer data relationships differ in test design and method of execution.

In the *sequential* approach, the two studies whose data will be related are conducted sequentially. This approach is used frequently by sensory professionals in routine testing. One test (usually a discrimination or descriptive test) is completed first, results are analyzed and interpreted, and, if required, a consumer test is conducted thereafter. The analysis of data relationships is completed once both data sets are collected. The analysis may be only qualitative or univariate, since the number of products tested in this approach is usually limited.

Shelf life studies, which use descriptive and consumer tests, are examples of sequential data relationships studies. First, a descriptive test is conducted to characterize the differences between the test and control products. If results show large and/or significant descriptive differences, a consumer study is designed and conducted. Both sets of data (i.e., descriptive and consumer) are related to understand the effect of product differences, as measured by a descriptive panel, on consumer acceptance.

In the *simultaneous* approach, all tests are designed and conducted simultaneously. The design is specifically geared to study data relationships, and therefore the test samples are chosen to encompass the variables and relationships of interest. The laboratory/analytical (e.g., descriptive) and consumer tests are conducted simultaneously to generate the required data, and to complete the data relationship analysis. The simultaneous approach represents the most effective method to study data relationships, since many variables and relationships of interest are studied in one comprehensive test, as compared to the sequential approach, where only a few variables and relationships are studied at a time. The analysis in the simultaneous approach is more complex, and multivariate methods may be used, since a large product set is usually tested.

TABLE 1—*Types of consumer data relationships.*

Group	Type	Classification Based on
I	sequential simultaneous	test design and execution
II	consumer-descriptive consumer-instrumental consumer-ingredients consumer-consumer factors consumer-employee consumer	type of information related to consumer information
III	interpretive predictive	use of data relationships information

B. Specific Consumer Data Relationships

This classification is based on the type of information related to consumer responses (Table 1).

Consumer-descriptive data relationships involve the use of descriptive analysis and consumer data. Descriptive analysis data, generated by a highly trained descriptive panel, provide information on the perceived sensory attributes (e.g., appearance, flavor, fragrance, skinfeel) and their intensities. These data are related to consumer responses, such as consumer acceptance and diagnostics (attribute intensities rated by consumers). These data relationship results are used to interpret and to predict consumer responses based on trained panel data.

Consumer-instrumental data relationships relate consumer responses (e.g., consumer acceptance and diagnostics) to instrumental measurements such as physical and chemical data. If a descriptive panel is available, it is also desirable to collect descriptive measurements to aid in the understanding and interpretation of the consumer-instrumental relationships.

Consumer ingredients and *consumer-process data relationships* relate consumer responses to ingredient or processing variations. The consumer data are obtained from a consumer study. The ingredient or process data are the different levels of ingredients or process conditions used to produce the test products. The relationship is built to study how varying levels of ingredients or process conditions affect consumer responses (e.g., acceptance or diagnostics) and/or to predict consumer responses to products that have not been physically tested. Optimization studies fall into this category, in which a relationship is built to study how a consumer response (e.g., acceptance) varies as a function of different combinations and levels of ingredients or processing conditions. The data relationship analysis shows the "optimal" ingredient and/or process combination that yields the highest consumer response (e.g., acceptance) [*2,3*].

Consumer-consumer/market factors data relationships relate consumer responses to information, such as demographics, (e.g., age, gender, brand usage), city, marketing data, etc. The main use of this type of data relationship is to identify subgroups of people (segments) within the consumer population tested and to study how the consumer responses (e.g., acceptance and diagnostics) differ across the sub groups/segments [*4*].

Consumer-employee consumer data relationships study the relationship between naive consumer responses (i.e., recruited from the population of product users not associated with the company) and employee consumer responses (i.e., employees within a corporation who are also product users). The main use of this type of data relationship is to predict the naive/actual consumer response based on internal employee consumer data.

C. Interpretive and predictive consumer data relationships

This classification is based on how the results of consumer data relationships are used.

Interpretive consumer data relationships studies are designed to provide a better understanding and interpretation of consumer responses. In some cases, consumer data alone: (1) do not provide the specific guidance researchers need, and (2) may be sometimes misleading if used and interpreted by themselves [*1*].

Some consumer responses need to be interpreted through more specific and precise product information (e.g., descriptive, instrumental) since consumers are not, and should not be, trained to provide descriptive product information. A trained descriptive panel, due to its training, provides more specific product information. According to Muñoz and Chambers [*1*], consumer attribute information:

- may not be technical and specific enough for research guidance
- may be integrated (i.e., several product attributes are combined into one term, such as "creamy," "refreshing")

- may be affected not only by intensities of the product's characteristics but by other factors, such as consumer liking, expectations, etc.

When specific and precise product information, such as descriptive data from a trained panel, is related to consumer data, consumer responses can be more fully interpreted and understood.

Predictive consumer data relationships generate a model used to predict a consumer response based on another data set [*5*]. Acceptance/liking responses are the most common responses to predict. The data sets used to predict consumer responses may have one or more of the following characteristics to be valuable for predictive purposes:

- provide specific and detailed product information
- are more precise and accurate
- are less expensive and time consuming to collect, compared to consumer responses

The most common predictive data sets in consumer data relationships are descriptive, instrumental, and employee consumer data.

Several studies are required to develop a predictive consumer data relationship model. The first study is conducted to collect the data used to develop the predictive model. The consumer data are the dependent responses, and the analytical data (e.g., descriptive results) are the independent responses. A second study is conducted to validate the predictive model. In this validation study, new samples not used in the first study are tested. The actual consumer responses from the validation study are compared to the predicted consumer responses to assess the reliability of the predictive model. Once the model is validated, it can be used for predictive purposes.

III. Applications

The most important applications of consumer data relationships results are:

- to provide more specific product guidance through consumer-descriptive relationships
- to achieve a more thorough interpretation and understanding of consumer responses
- to enable the prediction of consumer responses based on internal data (e.g., descriptive, instrumental, "employee consumer")
- to study different consumer segments

A. Specific Product Guidance Through Consumer-Descriptive Relationships

Consumer data are used to make product decisions, especially in the area of product maintenance, development, and improvement. Consumer liking results are used to determine if a product achieved the desired level of acceptance (e.g., an acceptance score of "8" on a 10-point liking scale, an acceptance score higher than the competitor, etc.). Consumer attribute information (diagnostics) is collected to investigate consumer perceptions of a product and/or for guidance to reformulate a product (e.g., if the product is "too sweet," "too shiny," "too scratchy," as perceived by consumers). However, given the simple terms/words needed to be used with consumers, sometimes the direction obtained may not be specific enough or may be misleading if consumer results are used directly.

Not Specific/Actionable Enough. Consumers are able to express how much they like or dislike a product, but at times may not be able to describe their specific likes and dislikes, and therefore may not provide very specific information on the types of changes a product needs to increase its liking. Consumers are not, and should not be, trained people as are descriptive panelists. However, more specific direction can be obtained by decoding consumer liking and consumer attribute data through the study of consumer-laboratory/analytical data relationships.

Overall liking. Specific and technical guidance to increase the liking of a product is obtained when overall liking is related to a descriptive data set. The guidance is therefore given in descriptive terms, not in consumer terms. Muñoz and Chambers [*1*] showed, through consumer-descriptive data relationships, how to determine the product category's attributes (i.e., hot dog attributes) that drive consumer acceptance of that product category (e.g., cured meat, moistness, fat).

Popper et al. in Chapter 5 illustrate this application as well. By multivariate methods, several descriptive attributes were found to be highly related to consumer overall liking of salad dressings. To improve a product, researchers are given direction on those attributes that affect liking.

Consumer attributes—The researcher structuring consumer questionnaires needs to select simple terms consumers understand and are able to rate. Therefore, the direction obtained from these questionnaires may not be technical and specific enough for a product developer's use. For example, consumers understand and reliably rate the attributes "flavor intensity" and "bland." However, a product developer may not be able to know what exact changes to make to increase the "flavor intensity" or to make the product "less bland." Other examples of the lack of specificity of consumer terms are the "integrated" consumer terms (e.g., "creamy," "spicy," "soft," "refreshing"). These terms are very important consumer terms, are understood by consumers, and may be the key marketing or advertising product characteristics. However, for the researcher/product developer, results expressed in consumer-integrated terms are not actionable since they "integrate" several attributes. For example, depending on the type of product, consumer "creaminess" may integrate appearance, flavor, and texture attributes. Furthermore, there may be several flavor (e.g., fat, dairy aromatics) and texture (e.g., thickness, oiliness) attributes encompassing consumer "creaminess." Therefore, many product attributes could be changed to impact "creaminess" perception. As a result, integrated terms, although understood by consumers, are not specific enough for product guidance.

A consumer data relationship study, which relates consumer responses to analytical information (e.g., descriptive), can be used to decode the nontechnical consumer responses to provide more specific/actionable and technical information to researchers.

Potentially Misleading. In quantitative tests, consumers are asked to answer all questions in a questionnaire. This means consumers rate all attributes, those they understand and those they do not. If a term is simple and understood by consumers, the product guidance obtained may be reliable (e.g., "not sweet enough," "too salty," "not soft enough"). However, misleading direction may be obtained for several attributes if their terms are complex or too technical since consumers may not understand them and/or may give them a different interpretation. The results of those attribute ratings may indicate a direction, but it may represent the wrong direction. Once again, most of the responsibility lies on the researchers, since they select the terms to be asked in a quantitative test. They may err in either selecting a very complex term that consumers may not understand, or err in having missed some relevant attributes in the consumer questionnaire.

A data relationship study as described in this manual may be used to investigate whether consumer direction may be misleading. The research by Muñoz and Chambers [*1*] showed that consumer attributes not related to descriptive data (or other laboratory/analytical data set, if collected) may lead to inappropriate product reformulation, and therefore be misleading.

Their study showed that for hot dogs "consumer spiciness" and descriptive spice perception are not related. This indicates consumers are not responding to the product's actual spice composition and its perceived intensity in this product category. Consumers are most likely focusing on other attributes when rating "spiciness." Therefore, if consumers would indicate they want a "spicier" product, increasing the spice composition and perception would be misleading, since this change would not affect the consumer "spiciness" response.

B. Interpretation and Understanding of Consumer Responses

Some of the caveats of consumer attribute responses were already discussed in the previous section. As a result, some researchers choose not to ask consumers attribute questions. However, most of the time attribute questions are included in a questionnaire to investigate consumer perceptions of product characteristics and/or to obtain product guidance from consumers. Attention needs to be given to the terms to be included in the questionnaire, as discussed above. If simple terms are used, the information derived potentially may not be technical and specific enough, may be integrated (i.e., several attributes are incorporated into the response, such as "creaminess"), may reflect other factors, such as liking, expectations, etc. [*1*].

A consumer data relationship study shows which attributes are understood by consumers; and therefore can be used in consumer questionnaires to provide valid and valuable research guidance information. In addition, these studies also show which attributes are either not understood by consumers or have a different meaning to them. Caution is required in the continued used of those attributes and the interpretation of their data.

Popper et al. (Chapter 5) found that consumers rated the saltiness of salad dressings differently than the descriptive panel did. "Saltiness" for consumers was related to the perceived levels of mustard and onion/garlic flavor in the product (as perceived by a trained panel). Therefore, consumer "saltiness" information should not be used for guidance on the product's saltiness.

C. Prediction of Consumer Responses

Consumer tests can be very expensive and time consuming. The ability to predict consumer responses based on laboratory measurements is desirable on occasion in order to infer consumer information without the expense of the consumer tests. Data relationships allow the determination of such predictive models. Consumer responses (i.e., liking/acceptance, attribute liking, and diagnostics) can be predicted through laboratory measurements. These measurements can be either descriptive or instrumental (chemical and physical) measurements.

The development and use of predictive models requires caution. Users should be aware that the predictive model is only valid within the product space tested. This means that as long as the products whose consumer acceptance scores are to be predicted have variables and ranges that fall within the product space tested when the model was developed, the prediction results will be valid. Extrapolation outside the ranges tested is not advisable.

Rothman (Chapter 6) describes several univariate and multivariate regression procedures to build consumer acceptance models based on instrumental data. A variety of instrumental tests (e.g., Hunter values, % fat, % protein) were used to build predictive models for overall acceptance and consumer attributes of breadsticks.

Due to the expense of external consumer tests, many companies conduct employee consumer tests to obtain a reading on consumer acceptance without the great expenditure of time and money for a consumer test with naive consumers. The employee consumer database is then used to make some product decisions at early stages of the project. A data relationship study allows the comparison of employee data with the naive consumer responses. Predictive models may also be developed to predict naive consumer responses based on employee consumer data. Alternatively, other data relationships may be used to understand the differences and similarities between both data sets. Daw (Chapter 8) shows the techniques to compare employee consumer data to naive consumer responses across products and attributes. Her study showed differences in rating magnitudes and patterns of both consumer populations for some of the products tested.

D. Understanding Consumer Segmentation

Frequently, consumer studies are designed to study specific segments or subgroups of interest. The consumer recruitment is completed to obtain an adequate representation of those segments. Examples of those segments may be different age groups, ethnic backgrounds, brand usage, and gender. Data relationships allow the study and comparison of those segments and their consumer responses. If results differ among segments, separate analyses are completed and conclusions are drawn for each individual segment. If different segments exist, a company needs to select a target population for which the product will be marketed, or needs to manufacture different products for selected segments.

King and Heylmun (Chapter 7) discuss the importance of this practice and show an example of how these segments are studied through data relationships. Specific consumer and market factors explored to assess different segments were age, gender, ethnic background, frequency of use, and location. Some differences were found among some of these segments.

References

[1] Muñoz, A. M. and Chambers, E. IV, "Relating Sensory Measurements to Consumer Acceptance of Meat Products," *Food Technology,* Vol. 47, No. 11, 1993, pp. 128–131, 134.

[2] Box, G. E. P. and Draper, N. R., *Emperical Model-Building and Response Surfaces,* John Wiley & Sons, New York, NY, 1987.

[3] Gacula, M. C., *Design and Analysis of Sensory Optimization,* Food and Nutrition Press, Inc., Trumbull, CT, 1993.

[4] Moskowitz, H. R., *New Directions for Product Testing and Sensory Analysis of Foods,* Food and Nutrition Press, Inc., Trumbull, CT, 1985.

[5] Moskowitz, H. R., *Food Concepts and Products. Just In-Time Development,* Food and Nutrition Press, Trumbull, CT, 1994.

by Dennis Irving,[1] Jeanne Chinn,[2] Joseph E. Herskovic,[3] C. Clay King,[4] and Joan Stouffer[5]

Chapter 2—Requirements and Special Considerations for Consumer Data Relationships

I. Introduction

When establishing consumer data relationships, there are many requirements relating to the data sets being compared. These requirements pertain to the following areas:

1. The samples to be evaluated.
2. The sensory methodology to be used.
3. The physical/chemical methodology to be used.
4. The data-handling procedures.
5. The statistical requirements of the experiment.

These areas are not independent. Decisions made in each of these areas can affect all of the others. For example:

1. The selection of a particular set of samples may cause changes in the physical/chemical methods to be used if a physical/chemical method cannot be applied to all of the samples.
2. Certain statistical methods may require that the sensory and physical/chemical data be interval type or ratio type, again affecting the choice of methods.
3. The number of samples to be tested can affect the type of statistical method that can be performed. A minimum number of samples is needed for some methods, such as multivariate tests.

The best way to check that all requirements are met is to have frequent and open communications between all groups participating in the study, particularly at the earliest design stages. This will avoid later surprises, which, in turn, can lead to additional testing at a higher cost.

A brief discussion of these requirements follows. Special issues to consider in each area are also highlighted within each section.

[1]Research associate, Sensory Evaluation, Clorox Services Company, Clorox Technical Center, 7200 Johnson Drive, Pleasanton, CA 94588.

[2]Senior scientist, Sensory Evaluation, Clorox Services Company, Clorox Technical Center, 7200 Johnson Drive, Pleasanton, CA 94588.

[3]Director, Sensory Services, Joseph E. Seagram & Sons, Inc., 3 Gannett Drive, White Plains, NY 10604.

[4]Associate professor, Food Sciences, Texas Woman's University, P.O. Box 24134, Denton, TX 76204.

[5]Senior research scientist, Sensory Evaluation, Procter & Gamble Co., 8700 Mason Montgomery Road, P.O. Box 8006, Mason, Ohio 45040.

II. Sample-Related Requirements

A. *Number of Samples*

The number of samples needed depends on many factors, including the product space of interest and the statistical methods to be used.

In order to decide how many samples to include in a study, a large variety should be screened. Then, if necessary, some can be eliminated based on criteria mentioned in the section on sample differences below.

Simple relationships (e.g., the effect of varying a single ingredient on consumer acceptance) might be established using basic regression methods, which could require as few as 5 to 10 samples. However, most tests involve complex relationships that require at least 10 to 15 samples to apply the appropriate statistical methods.

Multivariate procedures require a large number of samples to generate meaningful results. The more samples tested, the more likely it is that the results can be generalized. However, more samples typically mean higher test costs. It is not unusual to screen 75 to 100 samples before choosing the 15 to 50 to be tested with consumers.

B. *Product Space*

Before any studies are designed, the product space of interest must be determined by the experimenter. Depending on the goals or objectives of the study, this can vary greatly. The first step involves defining the product type, the area around it that is of interest, and the boundaries of the product type beyond which the product of interest becomes another type of product. For example, is the study investigating:

1. All salad dressings, shelf stable dressings, all creamy style dressings, or ranch-type dressings only?
2. All beers, just domestic beers, or a specific type of beer?
3. All potato chips or just barbecue potato chips?

The product type itself can affect the product space of interest as well. If the product is being developed to enter a relatively new category, the number of examples of the product space may be smaller than with an already established category. For example, if a study was being designed to investigate a new product area such as "carbonated vegetable soft drinks," one would expect to find fewer examples to test than in an established area such as "carbonated fruit flavored soft drinks."

For most situations where the experimenter wishes to determine complex relationships between different sets of data, the recommendation of the authors is to select at least 15 samples for evaluation. Often, prototypes can be formulated to fill in gaps in a product space when there are few established products available.

In general, the experimenter should not expect to be able to generalize the results beyond the product space tested. Results are typically valid only within the range of products tested and should not be extrapolated without extreme caution. Thus, if the product space is too small, any relationships found will apply only to the small space tested.

However, testing a small product space is not necessarily a negative if the experimenter is interested only in the relationships between a few products. Another case where a small design space may not be a major negative is when the few samples tested include dominant market leaders in the category that are targets of the investigation. There are some categories where one or two brands dominate the category. In such cases, if the product-consumer relationships are understood for products from those two brands, there is a good chance to formulate a competitive product. However, the risk in such an approach is that the products may dominate due to non-sensory factors, such as pricing, distribution, etc. If this is true, the experimenter may miss an opportunity to enter the category with a superior product if only the two dominant brands are tested.

In general, the product space cannot be too large except in cases where the samples being tested are too different from each other and actually cover several *different* product classes (see next section). The major limitation on the size of the product space is typically the increasing cost of testing larger product spaces.

C. Sample Differences

Once the product space of interest is defined, samples should be evaluated that represent a wide range of sensory, chemical, and/or physical differences within the product space.

In general, it is most appropriate to select several products with clear differences. If there are samples that are virtually identical, consideration should be given to eliminating the redundant samples. If panelists have difficulties differentiating between many samples with very small differences, test sensitivity may be lost.

On the other hand, if the product space is so wide that it includes products that are in totally different product categories, the underlying models may be more complex than can be studied conveniently. For example, suppose a test was needed to relate consumer acceptance or liking to different formulations/types of vanilla ice cream. The study could be designed to investigate different types or brands of vanilla, e.g., French vanilla, products with vanilla beans or artificial vanilla flavor, or light vanilla. However, a single sample of chocolate ice cream would not typically be included because it is so different from vanilla that it could easily have unpredictable or deleterious effects on the study and the results.

The following describes one approach for selecting samples. Continuing with the ice cream example above, many brands of vanilla ice cream would be purchased. Prototype formulations could also be included. The next step would be to determine which brands are somewhat similar to each other and which have certain characteristics that set them apart from the rest (e.g., the presence of visible vanilla beans). This may be done in benchtop sessions or through descriptive panel work. Typically, ice creams would be chosen that represent points on different known product dimensions such as sweetness, smoothness, thickness, etc. This should define an adequate product space because these varying dimensions should affect consumer liking. A product range that does not vary in liking will restrict the range of the dependent variable and artificially deflate the statistical relationships.

D. Representative Samples

Make sure that the samples chosen are truly representative of the product. Tests performed with samples that are not representative can yield misleading results, which apply only to the exact samples tested (for example, a bad batch of the product) and not to the normal product on the market.

Subclasses of representative samples is the issue of batch-to-batch variation or seasonal changes in some products. For example, a given brand of orange juice may be different from season to season as the type of oranges that make up the juice change. For such orange juices, one approach is to relate the samples to consumer responses during peak-, mid-, and off-seasons.

To obtain representative samples, the samples should be purchased from different stores in different areas of the country with varied climates. They should also be as close in age to each other as possible except in the case where age is a variable of interest.

If the samples are internally prepared, ideally they should be evaluated at an age (including handling or storage condition) when they will be available to the consumer.

Even if the test samples are chosen very carefully to be representative, an experimenter cannot always predict which samples will be "outliers." An outlier is a sample that is very different from the rest of the products due to one or several unique characteristics. As a result, the outlier will separate itself from the rest of the products dramatically. This can have unpredictable and/or deleterious effects on the results of the statistical analyses.

When an outlier is detected, the product characteristics should be examined to determine the reason why the product is an outlier. To evaluate the effect on the analysis of such outlier samples, the data from these samples are deleted and the analysis is performed again without the outliers. The results are then compared to the original analysis that includes the outlier. This allows a determination of how much the outliers are affecting the results. Based on this review, a decision must be made as to whether or not to eliminate the outliers from the study. Eliminating outliers usually has more significant effects on small sample sets than on large ones.

The decision as to whether or not to eliminate outliers is an important one. If the decision is made to eliminate outliers, the experimenter should keep in mind that, by deleting the outlier, the utility of the model may have been reduced. This is particularly true if the product area represented by the outlier is important to the experimenter.

An alternative approach to handling an outlier is for the experimenter to obtain or formulate samples to fill in the product space near the outlier and between the outlier and the main set of samples. In this way, the outlier is no longer as different from the main group and is thus no longer an outlier. Of course, this requires that additional samples be tested.

E. Sample Preparation/Presentation

Samples must be prepared properly and consistently by trained technicians according to package directions. However, sample preparation limitations may affect/limit the overall test design. This can occur due to the presence of significant preparation variability, sample holding times, or the need to take sub-samples of the samples.

The way the samples are presented to people may affect both the test design and the utility of the relationship identified in the study. Any experiment can yield only information about those attributes that are actually seen/evaluated by the panelist. Early discussions should be held when designing the study during which the attributes of interest are outlined in clear terms. It is often helpful to also create a list of those attributes that are *not* of interest. Such a list can often bring out those attributes that some experimenters take for granted and assume will be included in the test, but which require special efforts for the panel to evaluate. For example, if an ice cream topping is being studied, but it is put on the ice cream by a technician (not by the panelist), the perceived dispensing/flow properties of the topping could not be studied.

As in any study, the selection of carriers (ice cream for a topping, lettuce for a salad dressing) can also have an effect on the design of the study and the utility of the results. This is especially the case if the carriers themselves have the potential for major variability (such as lettuce). Again, any necessary carriers should be discussed during the planning stage, and any limitations caused by the carrier should be clearly identified.

In general, the sample portion size is kept constant in a test (unless that is one of the variables being tested). This is an important decision that can affect other factors, such as the number of samples that be evaluated at a time. A starting point for determining the sample portion size is the serving size recommended on the package. There are products that do not have nutritional or informational labels, such as wines or other spirits. For these products, present enough to panelists and consumers so that they may make a fair judgment. However, other sample portion sizes may also be appropriate. The experimenter may make the final decision, or the portion size can be discussed and chosen at a panel screening or discussion sessions.

F. Number of Samples Handled at a Sitting

Since studies to determine data relationships often have many samples, the number of test samples that should be presented in a given test session is typically a key decision. This is a function of the type of both the product being tested and the evaluation method.

The actual number of samples per session often depends upon how quickly the senses of panelists become fatigued. Products that present carryover effects can affect the number of samples per sitting. These include:

1. Foods that have intense flavors and aromas that are spicy and/or difficult to remove from the palate.
2. Products that have physiological effects (cigarettes, beverages with alcohol).
3. Personal care products that are evaluated by applying them to the body, such as hair care products, lotions, perfumes.
4. Oral, personal, or health care products such as cough syrup or some toothpastes.

In some cases, steps can be taken by the experimenter to reduce the above carryover effects and thus increase the number of samples that can be evaluated. For taste tests, the use of mouth cleansers such as crackers or water may increase the number of samples that can be evaluated. In odor evaluations, having the panelists sniff a neutral substance or having them wait between samples may help panelists handle more samples at a given sitting. However, some products such as lotions or perfumes may be difficult or impossible to remove in a short time.

Other than the above carryover effects, some products can also have product exposure limits that will bring with them a limit on the number of samples.

Product screening (benchtopping) is often an important step in determining how many samples panelists can handle per sitting. For trained panelists, discussion sessions can be held with the panelists to determine the number.

III. Sensory Methodology

A key to determining valid, reproducible relationships is in the use of sound evaluation methodologies for sensory tests. All of the general principles of testing (coding, sample presentation, randomization, avoiding bias, etc.) should be applied.

Since these tests are often large (15 or more samples), there is a tendency to consider cutting back on rigorous testing details (randomization, replication, etc). Such shortcuts should be avoided whenever possible as they can introduce biases in the data that can show up as a bias in the overall model, reducing the value of the results of the model.

A. Consumer Testing

In tests using consumers, one role of sensory personnel is to ascertain that products representing differences in key product attributes are included in the test design. When attribute assessments are needed in the test design, sensory personnel input can assure that the consumer is asked to evaluate the attributes of importance in the product. Sensory personnel can also assure that the test uses a type of test method or rating scale that is best able to measure the attributes in the way needed to understand the product space of interest.

1. Experimental Designs—Sound experimental designs should always be followed and should be based on the test characteristics. They should include consideration of the number of samples evaluated per consumer and complete versus balanced incomplete block designs [*1,2*].

2. Variables (Attributes) to Be Tested—As in any consumer study, care needs to be taken when drafting the questionnaire. In data relationship studies, particular care should be taken to assure that all relevant aspects of the product are evaluated. These may include appearance, aroma, ease of handling or using, taste, storage, appeal to family or user, product life, product availability, and price. Not all of these will be important for every product or category.

3. Questionnaire/Scaling—Questions with most importance or having the most weight in the test should be asked first to achieve the most unbiased responses [*3,4*]. One of these questions will usually be overall liking.

Questions concerning the product attributes can be asked in a natural order of product use experience or by clustering according to like experiences. For example:

1. Initial color evaluation followed by residual color in an article of clothing after several washes.
2. Initial product container appearance can be followed by messiness of package container after use if the container is an integral part of the product.

Whenever possible, scaling of attributes should be the same format throughout the test [*5*]. For attribute intensity, 0 or none present/desired should be on one end of the scale and the most possible of the attribute at the other end of the scale. Liking scales, too, should flow from dislike to like in the same direction throughout the test [*5*]. For liking or importance scales, a "neutral" or "don't care" option should be considered as part of the scale to help determine the importance of the characteristics [*6*].

In general, specific brand usage questions should be last so that they won't affect the responses on product-specific questions. However, this is not always the case. In some studies, panelists may be prescreened for specific product usage prior to the test in order to develop information about a specific user group. In such cases, the brand usage questions are typically asked first. However, the experimenter should be aware in such cases that the product usage questions may affect the panelist responses to the later questions [*7*].

Employee panels can be well utilized to screen the questionnaire prior to the actual test. This "pilot" test will help flush out inappropriate questions, better define question order, assure scales deliver desired results, and provide reassurance that the important product attributes were included. Employees can be exposed to product arrays to determine if fatigue is a factor or if an array design is suitable for the test. Some products in the array may have outstanding or memorable qualities that bias response to any subsequent products. Employees can be an early warning system for such problems.

4. Base Size/Demographics/Source of Panelists—As in any consumer test, selecting the base size of a test is an important decision. Depending on the objective of the studies, different base sizes may be chosen.

However, tests involving the determination of relationships between sets of data may require considerations above those normally encountered in consumer tests. For example, there may be a desire to segment the consumer data in some way, which will require a larger base size to satisfy a minimum base size for each segment. Alternatively, the statistical criteria for projectability may require a larger base size.

Since these tests often include 15 or more samples, there are various approaches that can be used to obtain the data, but all products should be tested among a wide variety of consumers to whom the product is relevant. Ideally, this should be a nationally representative sample of category users; however, specific test objectives may lead the experimenter to test other populations.

In data relationship studies, segmentation of the data may be desirable, depending on the study goals. Types of segmentation may include region, competitive product users, specific life style, age, etc. In any case, plans for segmentation should be built in, not tacked on after the fact. Proper consumer test design should be used to obtain a usable base size for each segmentation group.

Employees are often used to evaluate product prototypes and competitive products. However, when a product field survey is desirable and data relationships are to be determined, employees do not represent a broad demographic dispersion of the population. Segmentation is not likely because base sizes are not adequate and population representation is not achievable.

Employees can also evaluate products not yet covered by patent clearance or too sensitive to release to the public.

5. Number of Samples Handled at a Time—There are many different ways to obtain the number of observations needed.

1. Each consumer can evaluate one product. This will require the greatest number of consumers. For 15 products and a base size of 100, this would require 1,500 consumers or more.
2. Each consumer can evaluate a subset of the products in a sequential monadic format as an incomplete block design. The number of product evaluations per consumer is dependent on usage period required, burnout possibilities, attention span limitations, and ease of product distribution. Each consumer should see a different product array assuring randomization conditions are met. While requiring fewer consumers, more planning and product assembly time will be needed to fulfill the balanced presentation designs, especially if consumer segmentation is desired.
3. If the usage period is short or adequate time is available, panelists could evaluate *all* products sequentially. This requires the fewest consumers. Depending on the product being tested, these evaluations could be performed in one session or could be conducted over a span of several days.

6. Reproducibility—Once the above are identified, the reproducibility of the test methods should be assessed by statistical means. Historical information from the test method may be used to obtain this information. If this is not available, pilot studies using smaller groups of samples and consumers may be run to obtain estimates using standard statistical approaches [*8*].

Evaluating this reproducibility information before the main study starts will indicate if the method is appropriate to use in a predictive model, as well as the sensitivity of the method. For example, assume the experimenter will be conducting a large, expensive test comparing two products with the goal of developing one that is different from both but between both in sensory attributes. The reproducibility information would be key in determining whether the planned test design will distinguish between the two test products. If this analysis suggests that the two will appear to be similar in the large test results, the test parameters can be changed to provide the necessary sensitivity.

B. Trained Panel Testing

The application of sound test methodology is key to a successful study of consumer data relationships. Several factors that are particularly relevant to trained panel studies of this type are discussed briefly below. For more details on appropriate methodology details, consult other publications on the subject, such as *Manual on Sensory Testing Methods, ASTM STP 434* or the texts listed in the reference section.

1. Experimental Design—Sound experimental designs should always be followed and should be based on the test characteristics. They should include consideration of samples evaluated per session, complete versus balanced incomplete block designs, and the need for replication.

2. Variables (Attributes) to be Studied—Product attributes to be tested must be determined in advance. If an attribute is not tested, the relationship with consumer responses cannot be determined.

Often, a key to establishing the relationship between consumer results and panel data is to have as complete a measurement of all product attributes as possible. This is often obtained from descriptive test methodologies using trained panels of panelists and agreed-upon definitions of the attributes. In such cases, it is important that the panel be well trained in *all* attributes being studied.

Once the attributes are identified, sample presentation methods can be determined (e.g., determine whether a technician or the panelist should put the ice cream topping on the ice cream).

3. Scaling—For many correlation-type statistical methods, the data from panelists should be from scaling methodologies (versus choice-type tests such as triangle or paired preference methods). Preferably, an interval or ratio-type scale should be used. Panelists should be trained on the use and the scoring of the scale. Reference standards may be used to anchor specific points on the scale to increase score reproducibility.

4. Training of Panelists—It is important that panelists are trained appropriately. Several training approaches exist depending on the test method used. Panelists should be trained on how to perform product evaluations. This will help maintain consistency across all panelists in their evaluations. Reference standards can be used to educate panelists on the terminology and specific use of the scale.

For further information on this topic, see *Guidelines for the Selection and Training of Sensory Panel Members, ASTM STP 758.*

5. Reproducibility—Once the above are identified, the reproducibility of the test methods should be assessed by statistical means. Pilot studies using smaller groups of samples or historical information from the test method may be used to obtain this information. Evaluating this information before the main study starts will indicate if the method is appropriate to use in a predictive model and the possible variability of the results.

IV. Physical/Chemical Methodology

Often, the use of instrumentation for evaluation of samples leads to consideration of studying new and diverse parameters of the samples. These include but are not limited to physical and chemical analyses. In this section, they will be referred to as physical/chemical methods.

An important factor in generating and utilizing physical/chemical methodologies is for the experts in these areas to work closely with the sensory evaluation professional, both at the test design phase and the execution phase. This close relationship can generate new ideas as to how the samples can be analyzed and can bring up any unique areas/issues concerning the data.

A. Selection of Tests

At a minimum, physical/chemical tests should be selected that are suggested by the sensory attributes and modes of evaluation (taste, odor, texture, etc.) being studied. This often means exploring test methods that are new to the company. Literature searches should be utilized to determine whether new approaches have been developed that are more appropriate for matching up with sensory attributes. If this approach is not taken, routine physical/chemical methods may be chosen for their ease of analysis or high accuracy rather than for the goal of exploring panelist perceptions.

A good rule is to do as many different types of physical/chemical measures as possible. Tests that are routinely performed on a given product type are a good starting place, but other tests should be investigated:

1. Tests related to all key sensory aspects of the product should be investigated (appearance, texture, odor, taste, etc).
2. The physical/chemical test conditions should be examined versus the sensory method used for panels (e.g., if the panelists drink a beverage through a straw, physical test methods should include some flow-type viscosity measures).

In selecting physical/chemical methods:

1. The physical/chemical methods should be able to be performed on all of the test samples. Some product attributes (products with chunks) may prevent certain methods to be performed on some samples. This may limit the ability to use the data from the method in a predictive model.
2. For each test method, the data should be classified as to its type (nominal, ordinal, interval). This may impact the type of data analysis that can be performed.

Physical/chemical information also may include formula information. When competitive products are included in test designs, however, a complete formula is not typically available. In such cases, selected tests can often provide ingredient information on at least some of the key ingredients, which can be built into the model.

B. Selection of Samples

The same samples tested by the panels should be used for physical/chemical tests. Samples should be tested at the same time as the panel. In general, the temptation to use historical data on a sample should be avoided. Unknown sources of sample variability (batch-to-batch variability, seasonality of the product, unknown formula changes) may reduce the usefulness of any historical physical/chemical data.

Appropriate sampling procedures should be used to assure that representative samples are tested, as is done in the sensory portion of the study.

C. Reproducibility of Physical/Chemical Method

As in the sensory testing, the reproducibility of the physical/chemical methods should be assessed. This includes statistical evaluation of accuracy and precision. This will indicate, in advance, if the method is appropriate to use in a predictive model.

V. Data Entry/Analysis Capability

A. Data Management

Studies to determine relationships often are very large, with large amounts of data. Some advance planning around handling the data can avoid trouble later.

Data often come from at least three different sources: sensory groups, chemistry or physical property measurement groups, and consumer groups. Each of these sources can have its own data format and software capabilities. Meetings should be held between these groups and the group who is to do the majority of the statistical analysis so that (if possible) a standard data format is used. This can include common sample codings as well as common output formats. Such advance discussions can greatly increase the speed and ease of the statistical analysis and interpretation.

B. Data Transformation

Both sensory and physical/chemical theory should be used to decide whether data transformations or data combinations may be worthwhile to include in the statistical analysis. For example, sensory theory about how a specific stimulus causes a panelist response may suggest that a combination of two physical/chemical test results (e.g., linear combination, ratio, difference, etc.) may be expected to yield a better fit with panel results than either one individually. Similarly, sensory or physical/chemical theory may suggest a mathematical transformation (e.g., log, inverse) of the data that could yield a better fit. In such cases, both the individual measurements and the combinations or transformation should be included in the statistical analysis where possible.

C. Statistical Analysis Capabilities

1. Need for a Statistician—Often, studies of relationships between data sets can get complex. It is important to have access to a statistician or someone with strong knowledge of the analytic method being used to investigate the relationship.

Open, early, and frequent communications with the statistician (or whoever is determining the relationship) is even more key in such studies than they are in day-to-day sensory testing. This is particularly true in the case of panelist-related data. Seemingly minor variations in how the testing is performed can influence the type of assumptions the statistician can make about the data, which in turn influences the approach to the data relationship as well as the predictability of any models that are generated.

The person should have a strong knowledge of the methods used in modelling data, as well as the possible limitations and pitfalls of each method. If the person performing the analysis does so mechanically, without such knowledge, the results can often be misleading since important indications of the value of the relationship can be missed. In addition, the person should be aware of and sensitive to the special aspects of testing with people (sensory data and consumer data). This includes the variability of the panelists themselves and the possible interaction between the samples and the panelists (such as context effects).

2. Basic Analysis for Each Data Set—Each group that participates in generating data often has its own methods of analyzing and reporting the data from tests that are performed. Before studying the relationships between the data, such analyses should be performed on each set of data separately and evaluated by the group that normally evaluates such data. This basic analysis can serve to identify unusual samples or patterns in the data (e.g., unusual distributions of scores in a given test method), which in turn can be used when studying and interpreting the relationship.

3. Statistical Methods for Relationships: Tools Needed—When determining relationships, a wide variety of statistical methods is used. For example, there is often a need to use multivariate statistical methods. Before the study begins, the currently available statistical, computer, and graphical tools should be studied to determine whether they are sufficient to provide the needed information. This early analysis provides time to obtain any missing tools and become familiar with them before they are needed. See Chapter 4 for statistical methods used for data relationships.

References

[1] Meilgaard, M., Civille, G., and Carr, B. T., *Sensory Evaluation Techniques,* Vol. II, CRC Press, Boca Raton, FL, 1987, pp. 83–106.
[2] Stone, H. and Sidel, J., *Sensory Evaluation Practices,* Academic Press, Orlando, FL, 1985, pp. 121–131.
[3] Amerine, M., Pangborn, R. M., and Roessler, E., *Principles of Sensory Evaluation of Food,* Academic Press, New York, 1965, pp. 419–420.
[4] Meilgaard, M., Civille, G., and Carr, B. T., *Sensory Evaluation Techniques,* Vol. II, CRC Press, Boca Raton, FL, 1987, p. 40.
[5] Meilgaard, M., Civille, G., and Carr, B. T., *Sensory Evaluation Techniques,* Vol. II, CRC Press, Boca Raton, FL, 1987, p. 39.
[6] Amerine, M., Pangborn, R. M., and Roessler, E., *Principles of Sensory Evaluation of Food,* Academic Press, New York, 1965, pp. 420–421.
[7] Amerine, M., Pangborn, R. M., and Roessler, E., *Principles of Sensory Evaluation of Food,* Academic Press, New York, 1965, p. 293.
[8] Meilgaard, M., Civille, G., and Carr, B. T., *Sensory Evaluation Techniques,* Vol. II, CRC Press, Boca Raton, FL, 1987, pp. 63–81.

by David R. Peryam[1] *and Alejandra M. Muñoz**

Chapter 3—Validity

A Note from the Editor (A. Muñoz)

Dr. David Peryam was an active member of Task Group E.18.08.05 on Consumer Data Relationships. He was actively involved in the meetings of this task group and participated in the development of ideas and the review of documents. In addition, he was developing this chapter on validity when he passed away. We, the members of this group, decided to publish this chapter as he left it, with added information from the editor to make this a complete document.

We believe this may have been his last contribution to ASTM Committee E.18 on Sensory Evaluation of Materials and Products, and perhaps his last written publication. As such, this represents a very important contribution and we are honored to be able to include his work in this manual. We will always remember Dr. Peryam and appreciate his contributions to this task group and to the field of sensory evaluation.

I. Introduction

Validity is a Holy Grail, a supreme and basic virtue in the realm of data relationships, research, and measurement in general. It is sometimes equated with truth, thus becoming the ultimate good, which is probably overstated. But researchers should have the concept of validity ever present, at least operationally, even though the specific term is not always used. Being virtuous, we know what we should do and our behavior generally conforms. So let's try to muster the facts and suppositions.

What is validity? There are many definitions available and the word is often used loosely. The basic stem of the word is "value." To be valid something must be meaningful or useful, such as a data set contributing to the solution of a problem. There must be true representation of reality, however reality is defined.

Validity hardly exists in the abstract, unless one equates it with truth, which would be self-serving and not very helpful. In practice, you cannot say whether or not a set of measurements is valid in the absolute sense. Any questions or claims about validity inevitably should bring the question, "Valid for what purpose in what context?" A measure can be perfectly valid for one purpose but not for another. One must consider objectives as well as applicability.

The intent of this essay is not to tell the researcher how to assure validity. It is highly dependent upon particular circumstances, and there is no single royal road. What we set forth is not revolutionary. Most people are probably aware of the points that are made, at least to some degree. Instead, the idea is to deal with attitudes, to generate understanding of what is involved, and to provide support for paying greater attention to the importance of validity.

To determine whether or not a measurement is valid is not a hard-core exercise. To be or not to be valid in the abstract is not crucial. Any claim of validity is always subject to question

[1]Deceased, formerly a co-owner of Peryam and Kroll, 6323 N. Avondale, Chicago, IL 60631.
* Additions to this chapter have been made by Alejandra M. Muñoz, the editor of the book.

upon the basis of the kind of validity or the criterion that was used. You have to get at the details, such as "Valid for what purpose?" and "How well was the purpose accomplished?" There is sometimes confusion between the concepts of reliability and validity, perhaps for good reason. The dictum is that a measure is deemed reliable if, upon replication, it gives essentially the same results as before. But a measure can be satisfactorily reliable even though it fails to meet the test of predicting a meaningful outcome in another realm. Simply by being reliable, a measure becomes valid for predicting the results of a replicated test. But this would demean the concept of validity. Reliability is certainly a virtue. It is necessary, but not sufficient, to achieve validity.

II. Primary Definitions

There are different kinds of validity, as one might expect in light of the many definitions of the term. It might be more meaningful to say that there are different ways of testing validity and talking about it. Alternatively, perhaps it is just that validity has different aspects depending upon point of view and purpose.

There is a central core of three main kinds of validity about which most qualified persons agree. These are described briefly below.

A. *Face Validity*

Face validity is sometimes called "faith validity," and perhaps for good reason. It is considered to be the weakest kind of validity testing. Yet face validity is pervasive, ubiquitous, the kind most often used, and often is given the greatest weight. Face validity is simply a matter of whether or not the model, the results of an experiment, or a set of relationships makes good sense. Would a reasonable person who is aware of most of the facts, factors, and assumptions involved be satisfied with the outcome or conclusion? Does common sense agree that the experiment measures what it is supposed to measure? Is it what one might expect? If the answer to questions such as these is "Yes," one has face validity. This kind of validity lacks rigor. It usually involves personal judgment, which is easily affected by idiosyncrasy and bias. To some extent it may deserve its somewhat tarnished reputation. Sole reliance on this approach to validity checking may mean trouble; however, the concept and use of face validity can be supported. It has a fully legitimate function as a sort of first line of defense. One should require that an experiment, a procedure, a test result, or a conclusion should undergo the face validity check, which could be considered as "necessary but not sufficient." If it passed, then inquiry should move on to a more sophisticated level. The awareness of face validity and the willingness to apply such a test are part of every scientist's repertoire. It is a fact of life and useful, if only minimally so. One should recognize its status but also be realistic about its limitations. "If you don't have face validity, forget the whole thing, but even if you do, don't go overboard."

B. *Predictive Validity*

This is the most solid and respectable kind of validity. Researchers like to have the luxury of dealing with it because it can be very clearcut. You know what you are doing. (Incidentally, the face validity of the approach is obvious.) Predictive validity has to do with the ability of a particular model or set of measurements, taken in a given situation, to forecast a meaningful outcome in another realm. The approach is rigorous and rule abiding. Usually the degree of validity can be evaluated statistically by correlational methods. An example of predictive validity would be evaluation of the performance of a small, in-house panel. How useful are the preference results obtained with such a group for measuring consumer preferences in general? The small panel results (predictor variable) are tested against the results for the same products obtained from a large group of representative consumers (criterion variable). If the correlation is positive and satisfactorily high, one may assert that the small panel tests are a valid measure of what they are intended to measure, with the degree of validity shown by the magnitude of the correlation. A similar example would be the evaluation of consumer testing that has aligned products according to their relative acceptability. Such alignment, the predictor variable, might be tested against a measure such as sales data, which most people would agree is a meaningful validity criterion in this case.

Distinction among kinds of validity is not always clear. Face and predictive validity often interact and may be mutually supportive. Consider a simplified example. The project team has been working to develop a sure-fire version of a new product, but taste test results on a series of prototypes have not been encouraging. But finally a break through! A small consumer test showed that Variant B was definitely better liked than all other available candidates. Management was convinced that the answer had been found, namely, the Variant B would provide the sought-for market advantage. Given the test results, in light of past experience the connection was just common sense. Expressed another way, the initial taste test results had *face validity,* supporting management's faith. So Variant B moved on to the marketing phase. But was the decision a good one?

Let's write a sequel, jumping ahead a reasonable length of time. We find Variant B going like gangbusters, its market share dizzying constantly upward. This is just what management had predicted based upon faith. Now, however, the earlier performance testing has acquired new status. By virtue of the crucial test of the marketplace, they also have *predictive validity.* A point to ponder is that when predictive validity has been demonstrated it often generates strong feelings about face validity. Hard facts encourage faith in "soft facts."

C. Construct Validity

Construct validity presents another facet. It is relatively sophisticated and complex as compared to the other approaches and, in general, is rarely involved in routine, pragmatic day-to-day operations. It usually comes into the picture in cases where the overall situation is complex, with many possible ramifications that require planning and effort. Inquiry into construct validity is a matter of examining the degree to which the results of a particular measure under consideration agree with the results obtained from independent approaches to the same situation. Stated in another way, one looks at the problem of estimating some outcome in several different ways and hopes to get approximately the same answer each time. The degree of agreement reflects the validity of all of the different measures as well as the validity of the construct itself. The construct is created either during the process or is hypothesized *a priori.* Essentially, it is the conceptual representation of a situation that has certain properties and operating characteristics such that certain outcomes can be expected. Development of the construct is based upon measurements done in different ways, but do the dimensions or properties hypothesized for the construct actually exist in the real world? All of the measurements that are taken should point in the same direction. If they do, one may conclude that the construct is valid.

III. Other Definitions

The above are the major categories for arranging the rather diffuse and variegated phenomena that are placed under the broad topic of validity. There are some other definitions that might be included, although in large part they may be mostly a matter of using different language.

A. Content Validity

One may ask whether or not the issues being addressed in an experiment are meaningful and appropriate. Does the test contain pertinent or useful items? Are you asking questions that can reasonably be answered? If so, one may claim "content validity." Obviously, however, this is just face validity under another name.

B. Cross Validity

The meaning of this term, as it is sometimes used, is not always clear. Apparently it has reference to the situation of determining whether or not different approaches to measuring the same thing yield reasonably similar results. If so, the validity of all of the approaches is supported. This seems to be a sub-category of construct validity.

C. Pragmatic Validity

Since any research study is designed to help solve a problem if the information obtained fails to do so, to that extent it is not valid. Validity is a matter of practical value. Can the results of an experiment or a set of measurements be put to good use? To the extent that they serve the intended purpose they may be considered as pragmatically valid. Again, it should be noted that a measure can be valid for one purpose, but not for another.

D. Replicate Validity

Use of this term does little more than emphasize the broad use of the concept of validity. No matter how well a set of measurements may seem to fulfill its purpose, if it does not produce answers leading to the same decisions when repeated in essentially the same form, it cannot be considered valid. A more common name for this kind of validity is reliability, as noted already. Let us reiterate for emphasis—to be valid a measure must be reliable, but reliability does not assure validity.

E. External Validity

In some ways this is like construct validity but at a less ambitious level. Its premise is that the validity of an instrument or set of measurements depends upon the degree to which the results are compatible with other relevant evidence. This is almost a truism. Relevant evidence might mean the results from similar, but not identical, measurement approaches, or observations made independently on quite different factors. The emphasis is on seeking for supporting evidence in an outside situation apart from the original measurements. Again, it may be noted that identifying the external situations that become validating criteria may require the reliance on face validity.

Additions from the Editor (A. Muñoz)

IV. Validity in the Area of Consumer Data Relationships

Consumer data relationships need to be valid in order to be useful. Therefore, researchers involved in the study of consumer data relationships should ensure the validity of their data relationships results by:

1. Following test practices that ensure validity of test results.

2. Checking the validity of data relationship results prior to their implementation.

V. Practices to Ensure Valid Relationships

A sound study is necessary to ensure validity of the results. In a data relationship study, the most important practices that a researcher needs to follow to ensure validity are:

A. Sample/Product Space

Valid conclusions from a data relationship study should be limited to the information provided by the test variables and chosen intensity ranges ("product space"). From the calculation standpoint, it is possible to use the data relationships results to predict a result that falls beyond the boundaries of the product space used to develop the data relationships. However, the results and conclusions from this practice may be invalid. Therefore, the design of a data relationship study should incorporate a careful inspection of the product space to be studied to ensure that the limits cover all variables and intensities that will be of interest in the future, when the data relationship results are used. The appropriate sample selection is one of the factors contributing to the development of useful data relationships and valid results.

B. Test Methodology

Validity is achieved by conducting tests using sound methodology. Data relationships involve several disciplines and/or test procedures (e.g., descriptive, consumer, physical, chemical). Each of the tests in the data relationship study should be executed with special attention to sample integrity, representative and uniform samples for all tests, adequate test controls, sound test methodology, participation of well-trained panelists and adequately selected consumers, etc.

Chapter 2 covers issues related to the use of appropriate methodology in data relationship studies.

C. Experimental Design

Experimental design concepts should be incorporated into the design of a data relationship study to assure that the statistical models and relationships obtained are sound and provide robust and valid results. For designed relationship studies, careful consideration to the treatment structure should be given to assure that the sample arrangement/design and set ranges will provide the best models. In nondesigned relationship studies (i.e., where prototypes are not produced following an experimental design, but rather commercial products or diverse prototypes are used), issues that one must pay attention to are: the number and distribution of samples along the intensity continuum (no clustering of samples), the interdependence of variables, the number of variables relative to the number of samples (important in some multivariate statistical analyses), etc.

D. Statistical Analysis

Incorporating experimental design prior to the completion of a data relationship study will determine the appropriate statistical analysis to complete. Collecting sound data through appropriate testing methodology and analyzing data correctly will assure valid results. The assistance of a statistician is always recommended to assure that the most suitable analysis is completed.

Examples of statistical procedures used to ensure valid data relationship results are: graphical inspection of relationships to properly interpret statistical results, techniques to compare results and confirm robustness and validity of results, appropriate regression parameters to develop regression models, tests to check overfit models, and cross validation methods for regression models. Chapter 4 discusses the selection of the appropriate statistical techniques for valid data relationship studies.

E. Validation Studies

Before data relationship results are used, a validation study is recommended. This study confirms the validity of the test results obtained through the data relationship models. A validation study is a small test in which measurements of products included in the original studies and new products are tested. The measured response values are compared to the predicted values obtained from the model. Very close values should result if a valid model was obtained.

VI. Checking the Validity of Data Relationship Results

From the several types of validity discussed by Dr. Peryam, five are important in the area of data relationships. The researcher should review the validity of the data relationships results before using them.

A. Face Validity

Dr. Peryam defined face validity as the degree to which the models or results make sense. The researcher involved in consumer data relationships checks the face validity of the results based on his knowledge of the products and the consumer population.

1. Relationships between consumer liking and laboratory data

The researcher can confirm the face validity of the results by studying the direction of liking with changing levels of the variables. In most cases, a positive relation should exist between the "on" or desirable product attributes (chocolate flavor, fuzziness in paper, rinsability is soaps) and liking, while a negative relation should exist between "off" or undesirable product attributes (oxidation, plastic, metallic, gritty) and liking. There are, however, other cases where the direction of the relationship is not known, especially in the case of a new product or new attributes in a product. Checking the face validity of the results in those cases is not possible.

2. Relationships between consumer attributes and laboratory data

Checking the face validity of attribute relationships (e.g., consumer attributes with descriptive attributes or chemical/physical variables) is more difficult, since the existence or the direction of a relationship cannot always by hypothesized. There are two instances when the validity of attribute relationships can be checked. One is when similar studies have been conducted previously and there is some knowledge about the outcome of the results. The second instance is when an apparent relationship exists between an analytical measurement and consumer responses (e.g., the relationship between sucrose and consumer sweetness; mechanical force/load to compress and consumer firmness; surface grittiness and consumer softness).

3. Predictive consumer response models

The face validity of consumer response models can be determined by assessing the sign of each of the variables in the models. An invalid model may be suspected when: (a) variables have changed signs from the correlation to the regression analysis (often a sign of high multicollinearity or overfitting), or (b) when variables in the regression model show a different sign than expected (e.g., chocolate level, or fuzziness, if they are desirable attributes, are expected to have a positive sign in a regression model constructed to predict liking).

B. Predictive Validity

Dr. Peryam defines this type of validity as the ability of a particular model or set of measurements to forecast a meaningful outcome in another realm. This type of validity is an important and necessary element in any type of data relationship. By definition, data relationships are used to understand and/or predict one data set based on another (e.g., understand/predict consumer responses based on descriptive data). Therefore, data relationships/models should only be used once predictive validity has been confirmed.

There are two ways by which predictive validity can be ascertained. The first one merely involves using statistical criteria to check the model/relationship and may not be sufficient to prove the whole degree of predictive validity of the data relationship results. Some of these statistical criteria are: inspecting the coefficient of determination (R^2) to conclude on the percent of variance of the independent variable explained by the relationship/model, inspecting confidence intervals around the regression model, or using cross validation techniques with different samples from the sample space to calculate their predictive values and compare them to their actual and measured value [*1–3*].

The second and most important way to check predictive validity is to complete a small validation study after the data relationship study. In the validation study, products not included in the first study (when the data relationship was developed) are tested. The actual measurements from the validation study are compared to the predicted values using the model/relationship. Predictive validity is achieved when both results, actual and predictive, are similar.

C. Construct Validity

Construct validity is defined as the degree to which the results of the study agree with the results from independent approaches to the same situation. In data relationships, independent approaches can be used in the data analysis phase to prove construct validity. Specifically, several independent statistical procedures can be used to compare the data relationships results and their conclusions. Examples of several methods used to reach common results and conclusions in data relationships, and therefore prove construct validity, are:

- use of graphical bivariate plots and correlation analysis
- use of several regression models and techniques to compare outcomes (see Chapter 6)
- use of several statistical techniques (e.g., uni- and multivariate regression analysis methods) (see Chapter 5, where PLS, Procrustes, and PCA were used)

D. Replicate Validity

This validity was defined as the ability to produce answers leading to the same decisions when repeated. This validity is important for any scientific study, including data relationships. A researcher involved in data relationships may have two laboratories (one may be his own) and conduct the tests independently (i.e., the consumer or analytical/laboratory tests). Data from the independent approaches should be similar to have replicate validity.

E. Pragmatic Validity

Defined as the extent to which the results serve the intended purpose, pragmatic validity is also a necessary characteristic of all data relationships. The results of a data relationship study are intended to study and/or predict one data set based on another. The degree to which such a model/relationship is used successfully for that purpose is an indication that pragmatic validity has been met.

References

[*1*] Snedecor, G. W. and Cochran, W. G., *Statistical Methods,* Iowa State University, Ames, IA, 1980.
[*2*] Draper, N. R. and Smith, H., *Applied Regression Analysis,* New York, Wiley, 1981.
[*3*] Martens, M. and Martens, H., "Partial Least Squares Regression," in *Statistical Procedures in Food Research,* J. R. Pigott, Ed., Elsevier Applied Science Publishers Ltd., England, 1986, pp. 293–359.

by Richard M. Jones[1]

Chapter 4—Statistical Techniques for Data Relationships

I. Introduction

The reader should be aware that this chapter is not a textbook in statistics or data analysis. It does provide an overview of some of the more common techniques used in data analysis, especially for data relationships. If the sensory professional is not trained in statistics, the help of a statistician should be sought in applying and interpreting many of the methods. Regardless of the training or experience of the sensory professional, it may be of value to combine forces with a statistician to obtain the maximum possible information from any study of data relationships as defined for this publication.

A. Data and Variable Types

The number and power of the statistical techniques available to examine and define data relationships is proportional to the information content of the data. Table 1 shows the most commonly used definitions of "data types." In terms of information, the nominal type of data carries less than the ordinal type, which in turn carries less than the interval type. Ratio data is a special case of interval data. For the purposes of data relationships, it is also useful to consider just two types of data:

- *categorical,* which includes all nominal data and some ordinal data
- *continuous,* which includes all interval data and some ordinal data

In that terminology, categorical data will contain less information than continuous data. It is sometimes possible, and useful, to change the apparent type of data by mathematical manipulation. This is called "transformation" or "re-expression." Although the information content may appear to change, there can be no real gain or loss. One exception is where interval data is transformed into dichotomous data and information is indeed lost. However, use of transformations is frequently made to allow application of techniques that would not otherwise be appropriate. A frequently used transformation is to take the logs or square roots of count data.

Table 2 is a matrix showing statistical techniques that may be used to locate, define, and examine data relationships for different combinations of data types. It is obvious that both the number and sophistication of techniques available increases as the information content of the data increases. There is some symmetry in the entries of this table. Any technique can be used, not only in the cell where it first appears, but also in any cell to the right or below that cell. There are some exceptions to that rule, and transformations may be needed to make the most effective use of a technique.

[1]Retired research statistician, 1810 Poplar Green Drive, Richmond, VA 23233.

TABLE 1—*Data types.*

Nominal—Numbers or symbols used to denote membership in a group or class. Examples: ZIP code, male/female, area code
Ordinal—Numbers that denote a ranking within or between groups or classes. Examples: preference, socioeconomic group, school grade level
Interval—Numbers used to denote a distance or location on a known continuous scale with a zero point which is usually arbitrary. Examples: time, temperature (°F or °C), age
Ratio—A special case of interval data where there is a true zero point. Examples: mass, volume, density

At this point, it is necessary to define "variable" and "variable types." A variable is anything that we measure such as temperature, liking, color, or choice. In data relationships, we basically deal with two types of variables.

1. *Independent variable:* a variable over which we have control and can set at one or more fixed points for obtaining an observation. It may also be an uncontrolled variable that can be observed easily at varying levels with little effort or cost. This type of variable is sometimes called a "predictor" or "predictor variable" because its value can be used to predict values in other variables. It is also occasionally called an "explanatory variable" because it can be said to explain changes in other variables.
2. *Dependent variable:* a variable that changes its value as a result of changes in the value of the independent variable. This type of variable is sometime referred to as a "response" or "response variable" because it "responds" to changes in the independent variable.

B. Computers and Software

Another facet of data analysis that must be discussed briefly is the use of computers and statistical and graphics software. Many packages are available that can do any or all of the methods discussed here. Not all are easy to use or "user friendly." Some care must be taken in the selection of not only the method of analysis for data relationships, but also the selection of computer software to do the analysis.

It is usually best to use familiar software, if possible. It is always best to seek advice from an experienced colleague if you must obtain new software. Some analyses return voluminous quantities of tabular data about the results, while others use such terse condensations that they are almost meaningless to most users. The old saying may be paraphrased to say that "all software is not created equal." Some of the best software is integrated so that several different analyses can be run without using several programs that are only loosely grouped as a package. Look carefully at what you have available before jumping into some "new and improved" software. Your results are more likely to be easily understood from software you already have and with which you feel comfortable.

Whatever software you use should have some graphics capability or should be able to transfer data to a graphics program. It is much better to have good graphics integrated into the statistics package than to need a separate graphics program. Regardless of how careful one is, the chance of error is always increased when data must be transferred outside of the program that generated it.

TABLE 2—*Statistical methods in data relationships.*

Dependent Variable Type	Independent Variable Type		
	Nominal	Ordinal	Interval
Nominal	Frequency tables Contingency coefficient Correspondence analysis	Frequency tables Contingency coefficient Clustering Correlation methods (Logistic regression)	Frequency tables Contingency coefficient Clustering Correlation methods Logistic regression Discriminant analysis
Ordinal	Frequency tables Contingency coefficient (Clustering) Nonparametric ANOVA	Frequency tables Contingency coefficient Clustering Correlation methods Logistic regression MDS* ANOVAs	Frequency tables Contingency coefficient Clustering Correlation methods Various regressions Discriminant analysis MDS* GLM*
Interval	Frequency tables Contingency coefficient (Clustering) Nonparametric ANOVA	Frequency tables Contingency coefficient Clustering Correlation methods Logistic regression MDS* (GLM*) ANOVAs	Frequency tables Contingency coefficient Clustering Correlation methods All regressions MDS* GLM* Discriminant analysis Factor analysis Principal components Canonical correlation

*NOTE: MDS = Multidimensional scaling.
GLM = Generalized linear model.
Parentheses indicate limitations on the use of the method.

II. Statistical Techniques

A. Graphical Analysis

Graphics methods are very powerful tools that are often overlooked in the analysis of data for any purpose. In the area of data relationships, there are many possibilities for the use of graphs. Something as simple as a scatter plot of one variable versus another may aid in resolving problems in the interpretation of a relation found in an analysis (see Chambers et al. [*1*]).

Simple scatter plots can also reveal unsuspected relationships. It is not unlikely that some important information could be overlooked if only numerical methods and results are considered.

The availability of plotting capabilities and good graphics displays within many computer statistics packages has greatly enhanced our ability to produce useful plots. Even when several variables are being examined, multiple plots of the variables taken two at a time are quickly done on a computer. Some systems even allow three-dimensional representations that can be rotated and viewed from several perspectives.

With today's computer facilities and statistical packages, there are few situations where graphics are not easily available. Given these capabilities, it should be made a general rule to do some graphic data displays and to use graphics in support of all analyses, especially in the area of data relationships. The utility of graphical methods is amply illustrated in the plots shown in Chapters 6, 7, and 8.

B. Exploratory Data Analysis (EDA)

Exploratory data analysis is a collection of simple methods both numerical and graphical to provide an initial evaluation of data. The origin of much of this methodology is in the book by Tukey [2] (also see Velleman and Hoaglin [3]). Examples of the analyses include many familiar methods such as bar charts, histograms, and scatter plots. Other methods such as stem-and-leaf plots, box plots, median polish, and the concept of data re-expression are also a part of EDA.

The operation of re-expression is also called data transformation, an example of which would be to take the square roots of observed counts to get the data on a continuous scale. All re-expressions (transformations) are reversible. This means that results of an analysis can be restored to the original units for final interpretation. The primary utility of EDA is to obtain a quick look at data to see if there are grounds for further analysis and to determine potential directions and methods for further analysis. EDA is particularly good at finding possible outliers and distributions that differ greatly from the usual assumption of normality.

C. Correlation Analysis

One of the most common statistical techniques to determine whether a relationship exists between two or more variables is correlation analysis. By choosing the appropriate form of this analysis, almost any type or mixture of types of data can be examined. For example, most of the case studies in this manual use correlation analysis. The correlation coefficient generated by this analysis can be used to assess the degree of relationship as well as the significance of the relationship.

The correlation coefficient is a summary statistic like the arithmetic mean. In other words, it is a single value that represents a relationship while conveying very few details about the nature of the relationship. By graphing the independent and dependent variables, the nature of the relationship can be visualized. In some cases this may lead to new ways of thinking about the relationship. For example, a graph might show that the dependent variable changes in a curvilinear manner, indicating a nonlinear relationship, even though the usual assumption in determining the correlation coefficient is a straight line or linear relationship. Any time a correlation coefficient is calculated, a graph should be made to obtain a view of the relationship between the variables.

Quite frequently, an unwarranted leap of faith is made in the interpretation of correlation coefficients, and a "cause and effect" relationship is inferred. The existence of a high degree of correlation and a low probability of that correlation having occurred by chance *does not* establish a causal relationship. The literature is full of both humorous and serious examples of authors declaring that there is clear evidence that "x causes y" simply because x has a large and statistically significant correlation with y. Such an inference can be drawn only if the results come from an experiment specifically designed to determine a cause and effect relationship. In the absence of such a specifically designed experiment, the results are equally likely to come from a relationship of x with some other variable that is the true cause of the observed variation in y.

The following sections describe some of the more commonly used methods for estimating a correlation. These are brief descriptions and are not intended as detailed instructions. The reader who wishes more comprehensive discussion and methodological detail should consult the reference list at the end of this chapter [*4–9*].

1. The Pearson Product-Moment Correlation—For most people, this is known simply as the correlation coefficient. It is usually given the symbol "r." The basic hypothesis in calculating r is that a linear relationship exists between two variables:

$$Y = b_0 + b_1X + e$$

where

Y = the dependent variable,
X = the independent variable,
b_0 = the intercept (the value of Y if $X = 0$),
b_1 = the slope (or coefficient of X), and
e = the difference between the observed Y and the true value of Y.

In most cases it is also assumed that the data are interval or can be expressed as interval data. The values of r must lie between -1 and $+1$. If $r = -1$ then all of the observed values of Y must be exactly defined by the above relationship and must decrease as the values of X increase. That is, all values of e are 0, and the value of b_1 is negative. If all values of e are 0 and the value of b_1 is positive then r will be $+1$. Therefore, at $r = +1$ or -1 a perfect linear relationship exists between X and Y. If there is no correlation between Y and X, the value of r will be 0 and the other equation values may take on virtually any values.

Some other properties of the correlation coefficient "r":

a. An interesting and sometimes useful property of r is that $100r^2$ is an estimate of the percentage of the variation in Y that is accounted for by X.
b. A very useful property of r is that it can cover the case where X and Y are related to some other variable Z. By appropriate calculations, the relationship between X and Y can be evaluated independently of the relationship of both to Z. This yields what is called a partial correlation coefficient.
c. As might be expected from Property "b", it is also possible to calculate a multiple correlation coefficient where there are two or more independent variables. Similarly, a partial correlation coefficient can be calculated for each independent variable. By ordering the independent variables according to the magnitude of the partial correlation coefficients, it is possible to estimate which of the independent variables have the greatest influence on the value of the dependent variable. This can be of great value to an investigator in determining which variables to manipulate to obtain a desired response or direction in the data relationships (see Box, Hunter, and Hunter [*4*], Draper and Smith [*5*], or Weisberg [*6*] for a more extensive discussion of partial correlation coefficients).

2. Nonparametric Correlation Measures—The requirement for interval data may be avoided by using one of several techniques generally called nonparametric correlations. This ability to analyze data that are not interval in type may be very important in data relationship investigations. In many such investigations ranks or other noninterval data are likely to be encountered.

a. Kendall's tau

This method can be applied to data that are at least ordinal in type. As with the common correlation coefficient, there is an assumption that a linear relation exists between the dependent and independent variables. The difference with Kendall's tau is that the relationship is between the ranks of the two variables. A simple explanation of the method and some of the advantages and disadvantages can be found in Siegel [*10*]. Like the usual correlation coefficient, Kendall's tau can be extended to multivariate situations. Tied ranks can pose some problems in both the calculations and the effectiveness of the correlation measure. The reference should be consulted for appropriate methods to deal with ties (see also Hollander and Wolfe [*11*]).

There is a method derived from Kendall's tau called Kendall's W that can be used to evaluate relationships among several dependent and independent variables in a true multiple association test. Like tau, this test requires at least ordinal data. The above-cited book by Siegel [*10*] has details of this method. Because it is a true multivariate method, Kendall's W can be a very useful tool in the examination of data relationships where it is likely that several dependent and independent variables may need to be considered simultaneously.

b. Spearman Rank Correlation

This method also uses rank data or data that can be converted to ranks. As with tau, tied ranks can be troublesome but are allowed. The major drawback to the Spearman test is that it is only useful for two variables. This limits the usefulness of the method in most data relationships studies. This method is also well explained in Siegel [*10*].

c. The Contingency Coefficient

The contingency coefficient, *C*, is another measure of correlation. It is derived from Chi-squared. Because of the derivation from Chi-squared, *C* is one of the most broadly applicable correlation measures. This means that most data types can be handled in this manner. It is particularly useful when only nominal data are available. Almost any text on statistics can be consulted for details of the calculation of *C*. Although there are some limitations, *C* is relatively free from many of the assumptions that restrict other correlation measures. The contingency coefficient has a number of advantages over other nonparametric methods:

1. It is free of any assumptions about the distribution(s) of the data.
2. It has no requirement for any specific relationship among the data, i.e., the usual linear relationship assumption is not necessary.
3. Almost any sample size is usable and tie scores are not a concern.
4. Several variables can be handled to do multiple correlations.
5. It can be used when data have been transformed.

There are some disadvantages to using the contingency coefficient:

1. The maximum value of *C* is a function of the number of cells in the table.
2. Even a perfect correlation will never give the expected value of unity.
3. Values of *C* can only be compared if derived from tables of the same dimensions.
4. All requirements for a Chi-squared calculation tabulation must be met.
5. The value of *C* cannot be related to other correlation measures.

D. Regression Analysis

A logical extension of the Pearson product moment correlation is regression analysis. Using formulas readily available in statistics texts [*5,6*] or computer software [*7*], it is possible to take a series of matching X and Y observations and generate following equation:

$$Y = b_0 + b_1X + e$$

where

Y = the dependent variable,
X = the independent variable,
b_0 = the intercept (the value of Y if $X = 0$),
b_1 = the slope (or coefficient of X), and
e = the difference between the observed Y and the predicted value of Y.

In general, regression analysis is used for predictive purposes. This makes it especially useful in the area of data relationships. Chapters 5 and 6 of this manual make extensive use of regression analysis. To obtain the results from a regression analysis, the sums of the variables, their squares, and their cross products are obtained. Because of this, the results of the analyses are frequently reported in an analysis of variance table (see below and Chapters 5 and 6 for more details).

The results from the analysis of variance table yield summary statistics designated as F values. From the magnitude of F and appropriate tables, one can determine the statistical significance of the regression, the reliability of the correlation coefficient, and the significance of the various coefficients (e.g., intercept, slopes, or interactions) that have been calculated for the regression. This allows an assessment of the value of the regressions and their components. See the section on Analysis of Variance for a detailed discussion of the F statistic.

In data relationships, one of the most used forms of regression analysis is multiple regression. The section on correlation coefficient touched on the ability to calculate multiple correlation coefficients and the partitioning of the general correlation coefficient into partial correlation coefficients. This comes from the ability to evaluate all of the coefficients in an equation of the form:

$$Y = b_0 + b_1X_1 + b_2X_2 + b_3X_3 \ldots b_nX_n + e$$

Where the subscripts refer to the individual independent variables (X_i) and their associated coefficients (slopes, b_i).

Other extensions of the basic method allow curvilinear relations in one or more variables to be investigated and defined. Equations such as:

$$Y = b_0 + b_1X + b_2X^2 + e$$

$$Y = b_0 + b_1X_1 + b_{12}X_1X_2 + b_2X_2 + e$$

and their extensions can all be evaluated. Note the use of the subscript "12" to denote the coefficient of the product of variables X_1 and X_2. Those with some mathematics background will recognize the multinomial, polynomial, and quadratic general forms of the equations. Unfortunately, the meaning and significance of the correlation coefficient become very difficult to determine when these more complex relations are evaluated. Most of the more complex analyses described below have their foundations in the basic methodology of simple regression analysis.

E. Analysis of Variance

The analysis of variance methods are frequently not considered when working with data relationships. However, there are many applications where analysis of variance (ANOVA) is quite appropriate. Chapters 7 and 8 contain excellent examples. In many cases, other results of analyses are reported using an ANOVA table (see Regression Analysis and Chapters 5 and 6).

Anything but an overview of ANOVA is beyond the scope of this work. In its simplest form, an ANOVA is similar to the linear relationship shown previously for the Pearson product moment correlation. The analysis of variance is derived from various combinations of sums of squares of the experimental observations. The use of squares removes the possibility of dealing with negative numbers. If any initial sum of squares results from an ANOVA are found to be negative, an error in computations has occurred. The total sum of squares is partitioned into the sum of squares due to a relationship and the sum of squares due to random scatter ("pure error"). The sums of squares are corrected, in a manner similar to that used in calculating the standard deviation, to obtain a "mean square."

Using appropriate methods, it may be possible to examine several known sources of variation all in the same analysis. In the course of performing the partitions and corrections of sums of squares for such multiple source analyses, it may be found that an apparent negative result is obtained for a partition of the sum of squares. This almost always means that the relationship being evaluated does not exist, and that the partition may be removed as a separate entity from the calculations. However, checks should be made to ensure that no arithmetic errors have caused the negative result.

The test statistic used to determine statistical significance is the "*F* value." This is found by dividing the mean squares of each of the variance sources (also called factors) by the mean square due to pure error. See Chapters 7 and 8 for some specific examples of the use of ANOVA in the area of data relationships. Any of the general statistical texts in the bibliography can be consulted for a more detailed discussion of the computations used and the applications of an analysis of variance [*4,6,8,9,12*].

There is a distribution-free ANOVA, Friedman's two-way ANOVA, which can be applied directly to categorical data. A discussion and explanation of Friedman's method can be found in Siegel [*8*].

F. Cluster Analysis

There are many possible applications of cluster analysis to data relationships. Cluster analysis uses a variety of mathematical and graphical tools to locate and define groupings of data. It is primarily used for multivariate data and can be used to examine relationships either among variables or individuals. Because it is used mostly for multivariate data, cluster analysis almost always requires a computer. Many of the commonly used statistics packages include one or more cluster procedures. Clustering can be done by observations (e.g., products) or by variables. In the latter mode it would be possible to relate very different analyses such as laboratory methods, sensory analyses, and demographic categories. This would provide a means of classification of products by simultaneously considering apparently unrelated test results. The texts by Romesburg [*13*] and Hartigan [*14*] provide both practical applications and theory.

Although some clustering methods permit the use of nominal data, most methods require the data to be at least ordinal. All clustering methods operate by determining some measure of distance between observations or groups of observations. The most common measure is

Euclidian distance, which is analogous to simply measuring the distance with a ruler. Another common measure is one minus the correlation coefficient ($1 - r$). Whatever measure is used, the computations assign individuals to a cluster so as to minimize the distances among points in the cluster.

Some procedures start with each point as a cluster and join points. Other procedures start with all points in a single cluster and divide that cluster into other clusters. Whichever method is used, some rules for starting or stopping the creation of clusters must be established. Most programs have reasonable default rules that may be changed at the user's discretion. Graphic displays are almost always used to assist in the interpretation of the results.

Many clustering methods allow for the testing of statistical significance. There are some cases where such testing is neither appropriate nor useful in cluster analysis for data relationships. There are many potential applications for cluster analysis in the study of data relationships. However, it is not universally applicable and requires some skill both in application and interpretation.

G. Multidimensional Scaling Methods

Multidimensional scaling (MDS) methods cover a broad range of methods to condense data into more meaningful forms [*15*]. The classical definition of multidimensional scaling is a procedure that measures proximity of items in several dimensions and allows each item to be "rescaled" for mapping into two or three new dimensions that are composites of the original multiple dimensions. In the sense that it uses distances, MDS is similar to cluster analysis. However, it is much more closely related to the methods that are primarily used to reduce dimensionality, such as factor analysis, discriminant analysis, and principal components analysis.

Most MDS methods are capable of handling all data types. Some provide special options for the intermixing of types. Virtually all MDS methods require a computer. In fact, several methods have become best known by the computer package name (e.g., INDESCAL, ALSCAL, Procrustes).

The practice of mapping many dimensions onto a two-dimensional representation is becoming fairly common practice in sensory analysis. If the multidimensional space contains consumer or analytical data, or both, it is not difficult to see that MDS may be a useful adjunct to other multivariate methods in determining data relationships. An examination of the dimensions created by rescaling can give valuable insight into the interrelations of products, their laboratory analyses, their descriptive analyses, and populations used to rate or test the products.

The plotting of similar products on the two dimensions generally will show locations that can be used to determine how analytical data reflects consumer perceptions of the products. It may also be possible to plot the products so that the relationship of laboratory analyses and panel descriptive analyses are related or define product location on the "map." In this work it is obvious that various graphics tools are essential to help in visualizing the results for both the sensory worker and those to whom the sensory professional reports results.

H. Principal Components Analysis (PCA)

Principal components analysis is a technique used to study the structure of correlations among a group of variables. A simple correlation table may show that several groups of variables are related to each other more closely than they are to any other variable or set of variables. To visualize this concept it may be useful to think of the data as a swarm of points in space with its highest density when observed along one line of sight. This line of sight or axis is the first principal component. The equation of this axis will consist of those variables that do the most to reduce the variability of the swarm. The second and following principal components are selected so that the axes are at right angles to each preceding axis or component and produce the maximum reduction in unexplained variation.

Each of the principal components is a linear combination of some of the original variables. It is therefore possible to create two or three principal components that can represent as many as 25 to 30 original variables and explain in excess of 75% of the observed variation. An examination of the original variables that are grouped in the principal components may give meaningful insight into the type of variation being explained by each of the principal components. In addition, these groupings of variables can be graphically presented to show product separation in two- or three-dimensional space that can be visualized. Here, again, graphical presentation of the results can be much more revealing than the numerical results alone.

I. Factor Analysis

Like principal components analysis, factor analysis creates some small number of variables that can be used to explain the variation observed in the data from a much larger set of variables. Although the theoretical derivation of factor analysis differs from principal components analysis, they are applied in very similar ways to sensory data. In fact, it is not uncommon to start with a principal components analysis to obtain some insights that can be used to initiate a factor analysis. There are some cases where the two analyses may yield equivalent results (e.g., standardized variables without rotation).

In a factor analysis, the "factors" are obtained by mathematical operations that work with the correlations of the variables as opposed to the variances, which are more commonly used in principal components analysis. This adds the constraint of some assumptions (e.g., linearity) that may not be required in principal components analysis. In many if not most cases, the axes found by factor analyses are treated by a mathematical operation called "rotation." The rotated axes yield a better alignment with the axes of the original data. These new factors and axes lose none of the explanatory power of the original axes. However, because of the better alignment with the original axes, it is usually possible to make a simpler, clearer interpretation of the resulting patterns of data points. This is not a procedure that should be attempted without appropriate training or a statistical consultant.

J. Discriminant Analysis

Discriminant analysis is a technique for classifying an unknown observation into one of several known populations. In some ways it is similar to regression analysis. A "training" set of data is fitted to a mathematical function that will give each observation the highest probability of being assigned to the known proper population while minimizing the probability that the same observation will be misclassified. It is possible that only a subset of the original set of variables may need to be used to create a discriminant function. In most cases it is thought that the classifications of discriminant analysis are useful only to determine the classification of a new data set. However, it is a most useful means of learning how seemingly unrelated variables work together to describe and categorize not only new, but existing products. In the terms of this publication, the discriminant function may be a combination of instrumental and sensory data on several similar products. It may be of interest to determine which of the sensory and instrumental variables, when used together, do the best job of distinguishing among several different products. From such information, combinations of data can be obtained that will define the relationships of various products among themselves.

This type of knowledge would allow tailoring a product to better compete in a specific market. Similarly, when a new product is developed it could be determined whether there was a match with one or more of the products from which the discriminant function was generated. The sensory and instrumental data can be used to determine the closeness of match by entering them into the function and finding the probabilities associated with the new product having come from each of the known populations.

Because each observation is located by calculating a "distance" between it and other observations, this methodology may be considered as similar to the cluster analysis previously described. However, discriminant analysis is a much more mathematically rigorous method and is better suited where probabilities of group membership must be determined.

In use, discriminant analysis is less likely to cause problems for the less skilled practitioner than either principal components or factor analysis. However, by careful application, much of the same information can be obtained.

III. Conclusion

An examination of the literature of current sensory analysis will show how many of these methods are currently being used. Many of these methods are well illustrated by the examples in the case studies included in this book. Some of those studies have been cited in the foregoing sections of this chapter. There are new methods and new applications of old methods being created even as this is written.

Hopefully this chapter has provided an overview of the methods and applications of statistics in working with data relationships. If it seems brief and less detailed than some readers might desire, they are invited to probe deeper by reading some of the books in the bibliography and talking with other sensory personnel and statisticians.

Acknowledgments

Although this chapter bears the name of a single author, many people have contributed to it. The author is very grateful to all those who throughout the process have contributed reviews, comments, criticisms, and suggestions. Particular thanks go to Thomas Carr for his help in getting started and with later contributions; the Editor, Alejandra Muñoz, for her patience, comments, and general guidance throughout; and all the other chapter authors for sharing their work for examples of methods used and their suggestions about this chapter.

References

[*1*] Chambers, J. M., Cleveland, W. S., Kleiner, B., and Tukey, P. A., *Graphical Methods for Data Analysis,* Duxbury Press, Boston, 1983. An excellent reference on the various ways of presenting data in graphic form.

[*2*] Tukey, J. W., *Exploratory Data Analysis,* Addison-Wesley, Reading, 1977. The first book on exploratory analysis. This provides many quick and easy methods to get a first look at data and data relationships.

[*3*] Velleman, P. F. and Hoaglin, D. C., *Applications, Basics and Computing of Exploratory Data Analysis,* Duxbury Press, Boston, 1981. This is a paperback book that is a useful adjunct to Tukey's book on EDA.

[*4*] Box, G. E. P., Hunter, J. S., and Hunter, W. G., 1978, *Statistics for Experimenters,* Wiley, New York, 1978. A classic text and reference on statistics and probability for all scientists.

[*5*] Draper, N. D. and Smith, H., *Applied Regression Analysis,* Wiley, New York, 1981. One of the most widely used texts and references on regression analysis.

[*6*] Weisberg, S., *Applied Linear Regression,* Wiley, New York, 1980. This is another widely used text and reference on regression and correlation.

[*7*] Chambers, J. M. and Hastie, T. J., *Statistical Models in S.,* Wadsworth & Brooks/Cole, Pacific Grove, 1992. An advanced text on many multivariate methods. It is most useful if the "S" mathematics package is available.

[8] John, P. W. M., *Statistical Methods in Engineering and Quality Assurance,* Wiley, New York, 1990. Although not written for sensory professionals, this text provides a very good introduction to experimental design.

[9] Snedecor, G. W. and Cochran, W. G., *Statistical Methods,* Iowa State University Press, Ames, 1980. This is another classic text and reference. It has been kept up to date by periodic revisions and new editions. The 1980 date may not be the latest edition.

[10] Siegel, S., *Nonparametric Statistics for the Behavioral Sciences,* McGraw-Hill, New York, 1956. This may be hard to find because of its age. However, it has some of the best "how to" instructions in the area of nonparametric methods.

[11] Hollander, M. and Wolfe, D. A., *Nonparametric Statistical Methods.* McGraw-Hill, New York, 1973. A comprehensive text on nonparametrics. However, it assumes significant math and statistics background and may not be suitable for all readers.

[12] Meilgaard, M., Civille, G. V., and Carr, B. T., *Sensory Evaluation Techniques,* CRC Press, Boca Raton, 1988. The statistical sections of this book contain many examples and instructions for the application of statistical methods in data relationships.

[13] Romesburg, H. C., *Cluster Analysis for Researchers,* Lifetime Learning Publications, Belmont, 1984. This is a practical guide to applying cluster analysis and interpreting the results.

[14] Hartigan, J. A., *Clustering Algorithms,* Wiley, New York, 1975. This is the "original" text on cluster analysis. It is quite useful in learning the methods.

[15] Kruskal, J. B. and Wish, W., *Multidimensional Scaling,* Sage University Paper Series on Quantitative Applications in the Social Sciences, 07-001. Sage Publications, Beverly Hills and London, 1981. This little paperback is an excellent introduction to the subject.

by Richard Popper,[1] Hildegarde Heymann,[2] and Frank Rossi[3]

Chapter 5—Three Multivariate Approaches to Relating Consumer to Descriptive Data

I. Objective

In the course of product development, it often is desirable to collect information on a specific set of products from both a trained descriptive panel and from consumers. By considering both sources of information, one can often gain a better understanding of the sensory attributes important to consumers than can be gained by considering consumer data alone. In particular, the study of the relationship between consumer and trained panel data can provide answers to the following questions:

1. What sensory attributes, as measured by a trained panel, are important to how much a consumer likes or dislikes a product?
2. How does one translate the terms consumers use to describe products into terms used by a trained descriptive panel?

With answers to these questions, the sensory researcher can suggest product modifications likely to improve consumer acceptance provided that the descriptive analysis is correctly interpreted in terms of formulation parameters.

This case study[4] investigates several statistical methods for answering the two questions posed above. It does not cover all applicable statistical methods, nor are the methods uniquely applicable to the study of consumer-descriptive relationships; the same methods apply to the study of other data relationships.

II. Approach

A. Samples

Twelve honey-mustard salad dressings were evaluated by a trained descriptive panel and by consumers.

B. Consumer Test

One hundred consumers were recruited for a central location taste test in which they evaluated each of the twelve dressings in a sequential-monadic fashion over two days. The serving order

[1]Ocean Spray Cranberries, Inc., One Ocean Spray Drive, Lakeville/Middleboro, MA 02349.
[2]University of Missouri, Food Science & Nutrition Department, 122 Eckles Hall, Columbia, MO 65211.
[3]Kraft/General Foods Technology Center, 801 Waukegan Road, Glenview, IL 60025.
[4]The authors thank Doris Aldrich and The Campbell Soup Company for contributing the data for this case study. The identity of the product category and the attributes have been changed in order to preserve confidentiality.

was counterbalanced. Consumers rated each dressing on six 9-point liking scales and fifteen 9-point attribute intensity scales. The analyses reported below are based on means of these ratings.

C. Descriptive Panels

Following orientation and training, a group of ten panelists evaluated the twelve dressings for appearance (8 attributes), flavor (21 attributes), and texture (15 attributes). Separate panels were held for appearance, flavor, and texture evaluations, and judgments were replicated over two sessions. For all attributes, intensity was measured using an unstructured line scale ranging from 0 (none) to 15 (extreme). Ratings were averaged across replicates and panelists. Appendix 1 lists all of the descriptive and consumer attributes used in this case study.

III. Data Analysis Theory and Results

A. Bivariate Graphical and Correlation Techniques

Multivariate methods are best suited for studying the data relationships of interest because of the large number of consumer and descriptive attributes involved. However, bivariate methods can be a useful first step in exploring these relationships. To investigate which attributes were linearly related to consumers' ratings of overall liking, correlations were computed with each of the 44 descriptive attributes. Table 1 lists the descriptive attributes for which significant correlations ($p < 0.001$)[5] were obtained and shows that a number of appearance, flavor, and texture variables were highly correlated with overall liking. As a next step, graphs of these relationships (not shown here) were inspected for potential outliers and to confirm the linear form of the relationship.

Correlations can also be useful in the search for corresponding consumer and descriptive terms. When there are many attributes, as in this case study, the approach quickly succumbs to the large number of correlations involved. However, as a first pass over the data it is interesting to examine the correlations between attributes that one might expect to be related.

TABLE 1—*Bivariate correlations between descriptive attributes and overall liking.*

Attribute	Correlation
Lumpy Appearance (vlump)	−0.86
Cohesive Appearance (vcoh)	−0.87
Spice Complex (spice)	+0.91
Mustard Flavor (must)	+0.93
Onion/Garlic Flavor (onion)	+0.85
Honey Aftertaste (hnaft)	+0.91
Lumpiness (lump)	−0.87
Residual Oiliness (roil)	+0.82
Residual Chalkiness (rchalk)	−0.82

[5]The significance level was set conservatively because of the large number of correlations being tested.

Figure 1 shows the relationships for six such pairs of attributes. Several relationships shown in the figure are very strong, for example that between consumer and descriptive ratings of yellow color, thick appearance, and between consumers' ratings of honey-mustard flavor and descriptive ratings of mustard flavor (the correlation with descriptive honey flavor was weaker and is not shown). On the other hand, for the attribute of sweetness the relationship is weak, and in the case of saltiness, low and seemingly inverse. Contrary to what one might expect, the correlation between consumers' ratings of smoothness and descriptive ratings of textural lumpiness is positive, although not very strong. Other correlations would need to be examined to discover a stronger and more plausible correlate of what consumers mean by "smooth."

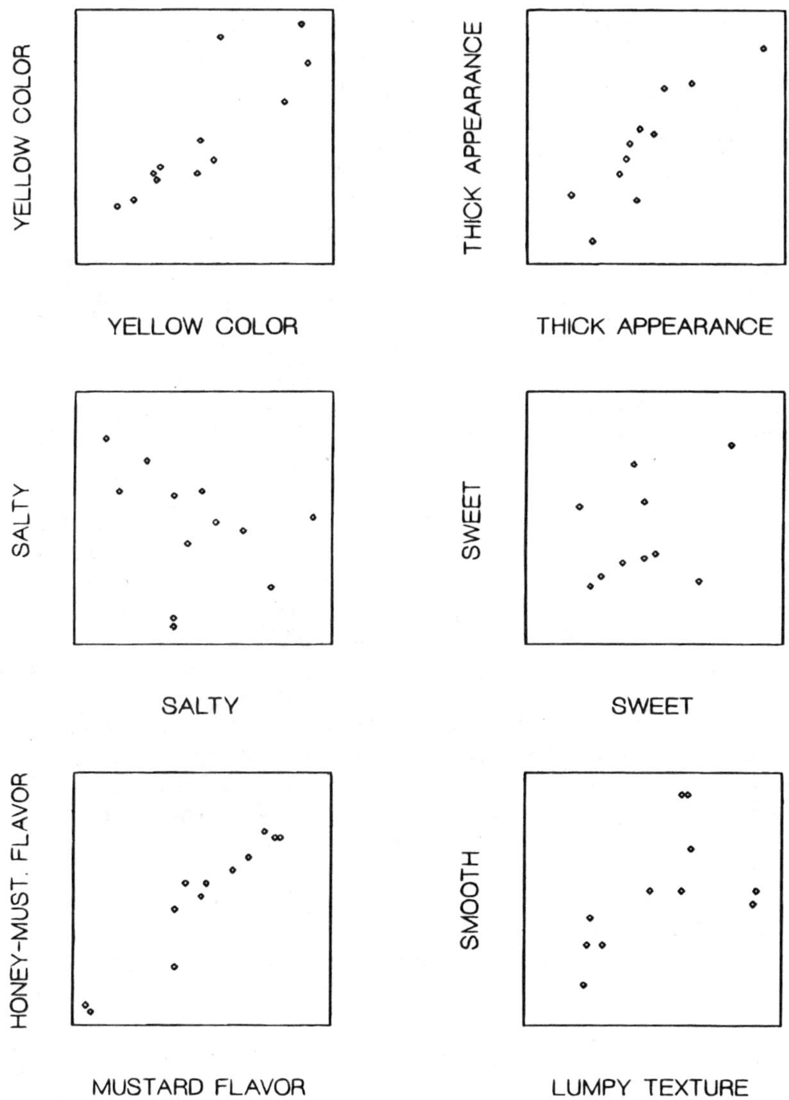

FIG. 1—*Plot of the relationship between consumer (vertical axis) and descriptive (horizontal axis) ratings for six attribute pairs.*

In what follows, three multivariate approaches to the study of data relationships are described, namely principal component regression, Generalized Procrustes Analysis, and partial least squares regression. The methods differ considerably in their analytical approach, and the agreement among the three methods, when used to analyze this case study, is considered at the conclusion of this chapter. In conducting his or her own data analysis, the sensory analyst might select one of these three approaches. On the other hand, using several techniques protects the researcher from reaching conclusions based on the limitations or idiosyncrasies of any one method.

B. Multivariate Techniques

1. Principal Component Regression—Theory. Principal component analysis accounts for the correlation (or covariance) among a number of product measurements through a set of linear combinations of the original variables, called components. Its objective is the interpretation of data relationships. It is hoped that a small number of components can account for most of the variance in the total set of measurements. If so, there is almost as much information in the small number of components as in the many original variables. Various methods exist to manipulate the components or factors[6] so that a better interpretation of each measurement's importance to the factors can be found. Principal component analysis is often used to create a smaller set of new variables for use in further data analysis, such as regression against other measures.

In this case study, principal component analysis was used to develop a set of factors that describe the correlation among the descriptive attributes. These factors were further refined and then used to predict consumer acceptance using regression analysis. The technique of first reducing a set of variables via principal component analysis and then using the principal components as predictors in a multiple regression is referred to as principal component regression [*1*].

Results. Table 2 shows the results for the first six (out of the possible eleven[7]) principal components computed from the descriptive data. The percentage of variability explained by each component is determined from the components' eigenvalues [*1*] and is indicated at the top of the table. The first six components together account for over 93% of the total variability, so the remaining components can be ignored without much loss of information. A useful tool in aiding the decision of how many components to consider in any further analysis is the scree plot of the eigenvalues (see Fig. 2). The scree simply plots the size of the eigenvalue on the vertical axis with the component number on the horizontal axis. The point where the eigenvalues stop decreasing rapidly is often chosen as the maximum number of components to retain. Here this criterion would suggest retaining only the first four components. However, in the present example six factors were retained since even factors with small eigenvalues can be important in subsequent regressions against other variables, such as consumer acceptance.

Table 2 also contains the "loadings" for the first six components. They represent the correlations between the attributes and each principal component and measure the importance of each attribute to that component. For simplicity of interpretation, one would like to see each attribute load highly on a single component. While this is the case for some variables, such as honey flavor (honey), there were other variables, such as spice/complex (spice), that load moderately to high on two or more components. When an attribute is associated with

[6]The terms "factor" and "principal component" are often used interchangeably. Factor analysis [*1*], an extension of principal component analysis, also attempts to describe the correlation structure of a number of product measurements, but using a more elaborate approach.

[7]The maximum number of (nonzero) principal components equals the number of products minus 1.

TABLE 2—*Principle component loadings for descriptive attributes.*

Elgen Value	19.13	12.18	4.46	2.19	1.84	1.18	
Percent	43.49	27.68	10.13	4.97	4.19	2.69	
CumPercent	43.49	71.17	81.30	86.27	90.46	93.15	
Variable	Factor 1	Factor 2	Factor 3	Factor 4	Factor 5	Factor 6	Attribute Name
HONEY	0.98	0.06	0.11	0.05	0.04	0.01	honey
PRTV	0.97	0.06	0.11	0.12	−0.08	−0.06	particle size variability
PRT3	0.95	0.12	0.21	0.08	−0.12	0.03	amount of spice particles (stage 3)
MUST	0.90	−0.43	0.01	−0.02	0.00	0.04	mustard
PRT2	0.88	0.04	0.30	0.16	−0.17	0.12	amount of spice particles (stage 2)
VTHCK	0.86	0.18	−0.30	−0.22	0.17	0.05	thickness (visual)
VSPC	0.81	0.54	0.11	0.08	0.05	0.09	amount of spice particles (visual)
SWTAR	0.81	0.54	0.16	0.03	−0.05	0.04	overall sweet aromatics
MOLAS	0.77	0.02	0.51	0.30	0.04	−0.09	molasses
SPICE	0.74	−0.63	−0.15	−0.06	0.09	0.08	spice complex
MSAFT	0.72	0.63	0.16	0.17	0.11	0.07	mustard aftertaste
SWEET	0.68	0.14	−0.66	−0.10	−0.10	0.12	sweetness
HNAFT	0.67	−0.66	−0.12	−0.12	0.10	0.15	honey aftertaste
ONION	0.59	−0.54	0.02	0.01	0.36	0.18	onion/garlic
ASTR	−0.60	0.12	0.23	0.48	−0.13	0.53	astringency
SALT	−0.63	−0.60	0.20	−0.24	0.23	0.23	saltiness
YELLW	−0.65	0.13	0.50	−0.13	−0.44	0.04	yellow color
SLAFT	−0.66	−0.25	0.21	0.07	0.22	0.52	salty aftertaste
BURN	−0.67	−0.17	−0.37	0.57	−0.03	−0.08	burn
GREEN	−0.68	0.09	−0.44	0.00	0.16	−0.02	green complex
VLUMP	−0.82	0.45	0.11	0.23	0.05	−0.14	visual lumpiness
VCOH	−0.90	0.36	0.08	0.11	0.09	−0.10	cohesiveness flow (visual)
DISAP	−0.92	−0.33	−0.17	−0.08	0.05	0.03	rate of disappearance
LUMP	−0.93	0.30	−0.15	0.00	0.11	−0.02	lumpy
PHASE	−0.95	−0.06	−0.06	−0.21	0.05	−0.11	product (phase) separation
COH2	−0.19	0.96	−0.16	−0.09	0.11	−0.07	cohesiveness of mass (stage 2)
COH3	−0.24	0.93	−0.12	−0.09	0.04	−0.01	cohesiveness of mass (stage 3)
OIL	−0.39	0.87	0.07	−0.16	0.15	−0.03	oiliness of mass
HEAVY	0.47	0.83	0.12	−0.06	−0.12	−0.01	heaviness
RCHLK	−0.55	0.81	0.06	0.05	0.14	0.02	chalky residual
THICK	0.58	0.76	−0.05	−0.12	0.11	−0.19	thickness

TABLE 2—*Principle component loadings for descriptive attributes—Continued.*

Elgen Value	19.13	12.18	4.46	2.19	1.84	1.18	
Percent	43.49	27.68	10.13	4.97	4.19	2.69	
CumPercent	43.49	71.17	81.30	86.27	90.46	93.15	
Variable	Factor 1	Factor 2	Factor 3	Factor 4	Factor 5	Factor 6	Attribute Name
PEPPR	0.64	0.65	0.24	0.09	0.05	0.19	black pepper
GLOSS	−0.55	0.63	0.15	−0.13	0.09	0.33	gloss
RBURN	−0.34	−0.60	0.07	0.51	−0.07	−0.04	chemical burn (residual)
OILAR	−0.52	−0.68	−0.11	−0.38	0.20	0.10	oil aromatic
SALIV	0.13	−0.80	0.15	0.14	0.18	−0.26	saliva production (residual)
ROIL	0.48	−0.86	0.03	−0.02	0.02	−0.10	oily (residual)
SPREA	−0.04	−0.94	0.24	0.01	−0.16	0.05	spreadability
SRAFT	−0.39	0.17	0.78	0.12	−0.01	0.08	sour aftertaste
SOUR	−0.18	−0.40	0.78	0.15	0.23	−0.25	sourness
CARML	−0.06	−0.20	−0.63	0.59	0.23	−0.02	caramelized
SWAFT	0.57	0.07	−0.74	0.08	−0.06	0.24	sweet aftertaste
OPAC	−0.23	−0.43	0.13	−0.46	−0.62	0.05	opacity
VINGR	−0.36	0.07	−0.45	0.29	−0.73	−0.01	vinegar

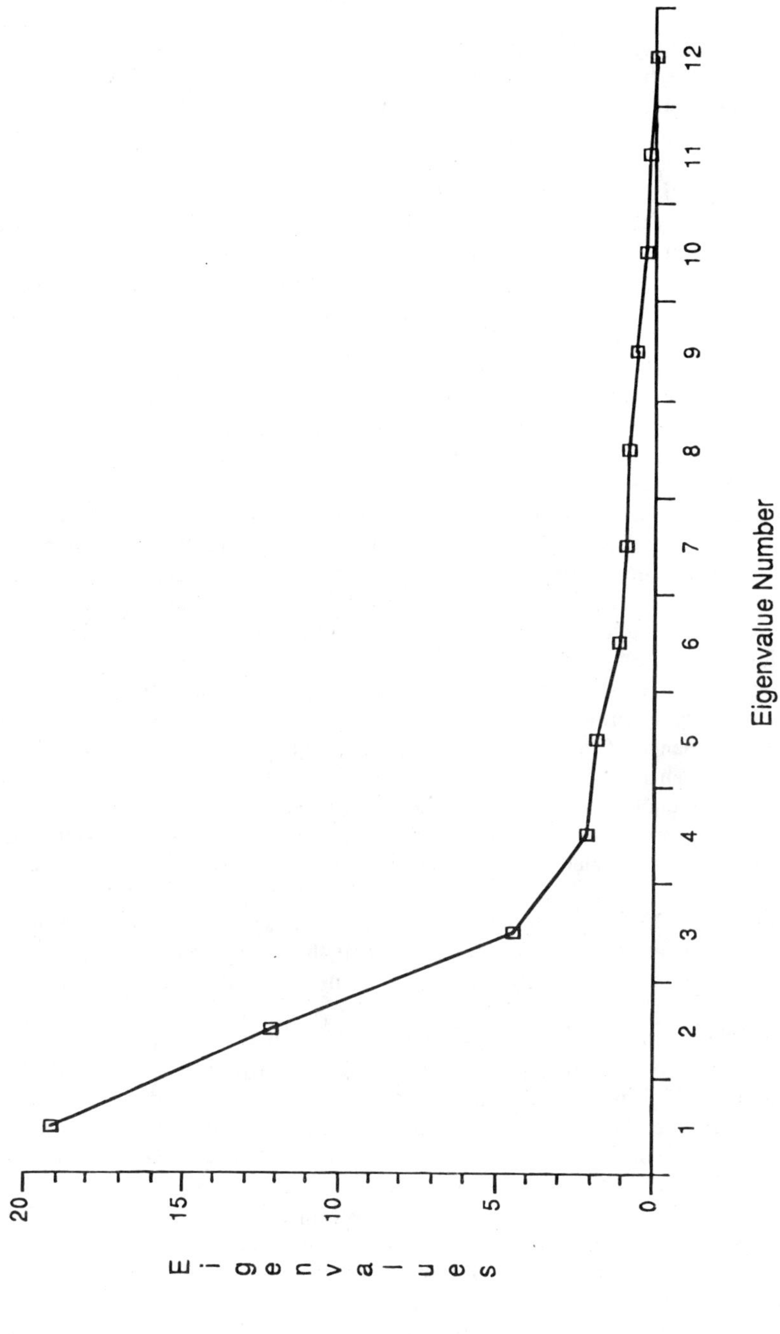

FIG. 2—*Scree plot of the eigenvalues from a principal component analysis of the descriptive ratings.*

more than one component, the interpretation of the components is less obvious since in that case any one component does not fully "represent" an attribute. Rotation methods will be considered below as a means of simplifying the interpretation of components.

At this stage of the analysis, a graphical technique can be used to gain an initial understanding of the relationship between the products and descriptive attributes. Figure 3 shows a biplot [2] of the first two principal components. These components together explain 71% of the system variability. In the biplot, rays extend from the center and are labeled with the sensory attribute names; the products (coded **a** through **l**) are plotted as points. Attributes that have rays extending in the same general direction are positively correlated; those that have rays extending in opposite directions are negatively correlated; and those with rays that are near perpendicular are essentially uncorrelated. Thus the strength of correlation between any two attributes is represented by the angle between their biplot rays. The *length* of a ray is proportional to the standard deviation of the attribute—longer rays indicate attributes with larger standard deviations. The position of the product points indicates how they fall with respect to each other and with respect to the attributes. By dropping an imaginary perpendicular line from each product to an attribute of interest, one can gauge the magnitude of that attribute for that product. For example, Fig. 3 shows that products **e, g, h, j,** and **l** are perceived as sweet and appear thick, that products **a, b, c, f,** and **i** are perceived as sour and salty, and that products **d** and **k** are perceived as oily with chalky residual. Some care needs to be taken in interpreting the biplot since the accuracy of the picture depends on how much of the system variability is explained by the first two components.

As the principal components are often not readily interpretable, they are frequently refined through rotation. Rotation does not change the total percent of variability explained by the components, but changes the amount of variation explained by any one component, increasing that percentage in some cases, decreasing it in others. More importantly, rotation changes the pattern of loadings of the components, i.e., the correlations between components and individual attributes.

Many rotation methods exist and can be performed using popular statistical software packages. These methods can be grouped into two categories: orthogonal rotations, which preserve the statistical independence of the original components; and oblique rotations, which do not preserve this independence. Orthogonal rotations are often preferred when the intent is to develop a set of independent predictors of other measures, such as consumer acceptance. Regardless of the type of rotation method chosen, a decision must be made as to the number of components that will be rotated. The number of components rotated, and the choice of a rotation method, whether orthogonal or oblique, is a decision often based both on the data and on past experience. Often, several options are investigated, with the option producing the most meaningful factor set chosen. The scree plot and the total variability explained by a certain number of factors are once again useful tools in aiding the decision of how many components to rotate.

Table 3 shows the output from a Varimax rotation of six factors. Varimax is one of many orthogonal rotation methods commonly used. The rotated factor pattern is now fairly easy to interpret. Factor 1 has high positive loadings for rate of disappearance (disap), visual phase separation (phase), oil aromatic (oilar), and saltiness (salt), high negative loadings for sweet aromatics (swtar), visual amount of spice particles (vspc), mustard aftertaste (msaft), and others. Factor 2 has high positive loadings for oiliness of mass (oil), cohesiveness of mass (coh2, coh3), residual chalkiness (rchalk), and lumpy appearance (vlump), high negative loadings for onion flavor (onion), honey aftertaste (hnaft), spreadability (sprea), level of spice complex (spice), and residual oiliness (roil). Similar interpretations can be made of the other factors. Note that following rotation, there are fewer loadings of moderate size (0.4 to 0.6) and a less ambiguous association of attributes with factor, thereby making it easier to identify

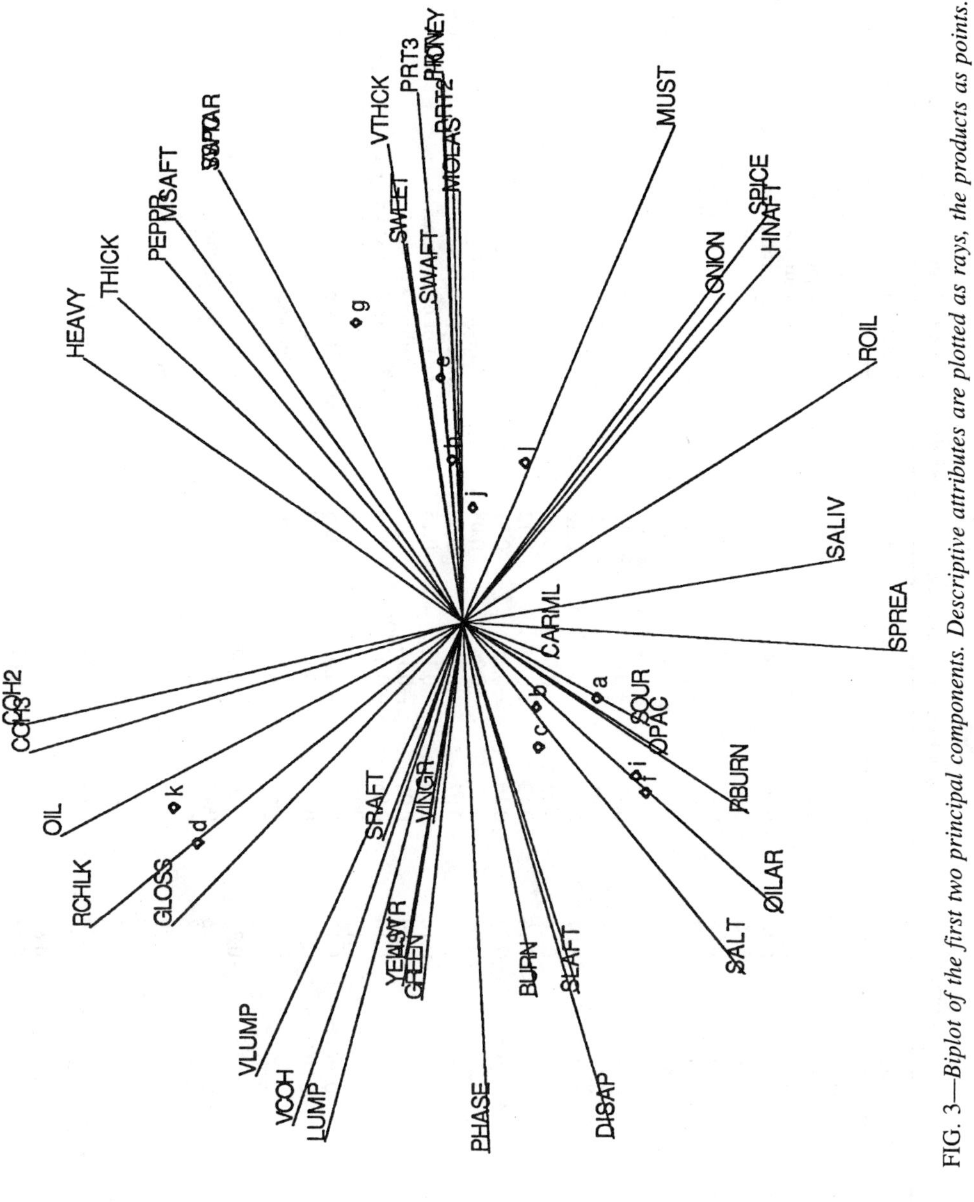

FIG. 3—*Biplot of the first two principal components. Descriptive attributes are plotted as rays, the products as points.*

TABLE 3—*Varimax rotated factor pattern and communalties for descriptive attributes.*

Variable	Factor 1	Factor 2	Factor 3	Factor 4	Factor 5	Factor 6	Attribute Name	Communalities
SWTAR	−0.94	0.14	0.19	−0.09	−0.12	−0.10	overall sweet aromatics	0.98
VSPC	−0.93	0.15	0.24	0.01	−0.19	−0.04	amount of spice particles (visual)	0.98
MSAFT	−0.92	0.26	0.14	0.10	−0.19	−0.02	mustard aftertaste	0.99
PRT3	−0.92	−0.32	0.14	−0.10	−0.07	−0.09	amount of spice particles (stage 3)	0.98
PEPPR	−0.89	0.30	0.10	−0.04	−0.19	0.10	black pepper	0.95
PRT2	−0.88	−0.37	0.05	−0.10	−0.01	0.05	amount of spice particles (stage 2)	0.93
PRTV	−0.88	−0.37	0.19	0.01	−0.07	−0.18	particle size variability	0.98
HONEY	−0.86	−0.36	0.22	0.00	−0.22	−0.14	honey	0.99
MOLAS	−0.86	−0.35	−0.28	0.09	−0.12	−0.05	molasses	0.96
HEAVY	−0.76	0.54	0.15	−0.15	−0.03	−0.12	heaviness	0.94
THICK	−0.72	0.46	0.27	−0.01	−0.22	−0.35	thickness	0.97
BURN	0.59	0.11	−0.07	0.58	0.47	0.16	burn	0.94
GREEN	0.67	0.39	0.14	0.24	0.07	0.03	green complex	0.69
LUMP	0.69	0.67	−0.16	0.12	0.11	0.12	lumpy	0.99
SALT	0.76	−0.26	−0.33	−0.16	−0.25	0.31	saltiness	0.95
OILAR	0.85	−0.35	−0.04	−0.17	−0.24	0.08	oil aromatic	0.93
PHASE	0.87	0.36	−0.26	−0.07	0.07	0.00	product (phase) separation	0.97
DISAP	0.96	0.10	−0.16	0.03	0.11	0.16	rate of disappearance	1.00
OIL	−0.02	0.96	−0.09	−0.06	−0.14	−0.03	oiliness of mass	0.96
COH2	−0.16	0.96	0.16	0.05	−0.06	−0.12	cohesiveness of mass (stage 2)	1.00
RCHLK	0.10	0.96	−0.17	0.10	−0.01	0.11	chalky residual	0.98
COH3	−0.13	0.96	0.13	−0.01	−0.01	−0.05	cohesiveness of mass (stage 3)	0.96
GLOSS	0.16	0.80	−0.13	−0.15	−0.11	0.37	gloss	0.85
VLUMP	0.40	0.73	−0.42	0.22	0.20	0.09	lumpiness (visual)	0.96
VCOH	0.54	0.70	−0.39	0.15	0.13	0.11	cohesiveness flow (visual)	0.98
RBURN	0.37	−0.45	−0.35	0.36	0.34	0.21	chemical burn (residual)	0.75
ONION	−0.23	−0.72	0.16	0.13	−0.44	0.08	onion/garlic	0.81
MUST	−0.54	−0.76	0.26	−0.05	−0.18	−0.12	mustard	0.99
SALIV	0.18	−0.78	−0.29	0.20	−0.10	−0.17	saliva production (residual)	0.80
SPREA	0.33	−0.85	−0.29	−0.15	0.10	0.13	spreadability	0.96
HNAFT	−0.20	−0.85	0.33	−0.04	−0.26	−0.02	honey aftertaste	0.94
SPICE	−0.26	−0.86	0.35	0.02	−0.22	−0.08	spice complex	0.98
ROIL	−0.03	−0.98	0.02	0.00	−0.10	−0.14	oily residual	0.98
SWAFT	−0.29	−0.15	0.89	0.20	0.07	0.01	sweet aftertaste	0.94
SWEET	−0.39	−0.13	0.87	0.04	0.02	−0.16	sweetness	0.95

TABLE 3—*Varimax rotated factor pattern and communalties for descriptive attributes—Continued.*

Variable	Factor 1	Factor 2	Factor 3	Factor 4	Factor 5	Factor 6	Attribute Name	Communalities
VTHCK	−0.60	−0.16	0.61	−0.02	−0.35	−0.24	thickness (visual)	0.94
YELLW	0.29	0.35	−0.56	−0.47	0.35	0.20	yellow color	0.90
SRAFT	−0.04	0.27	−0.79	−0.17	−0.01	−0.31	sour aftertaste	0.82
SOUR	0.06	−0.31	−0.89	0.05	−0.19	−0.01	sourness	0.93
VINGR	0.25	0.17	0.26	0.01	0.89	0.07	vinegar	0.95
CARML	0.22	−0.15	0.35	0.78	0.18	0.06	caramelized	0.84
OPAC	0.36	−0.30	−0.08	−0.71	0.34	0.00	opacity	0.85
ASTR	0.21	0.30	−0.32	0.15	0.31	0.78	astringency	0.96
SLAFT	0.57	0.04	−0.30	0.02	−0.15	0.66	salty aftertaste	0.87

which attributes are important to a factor. For example, the variable spice complex (spice) now loads highly only on Factor 2.

A measure of the adequacy of a specific factor solution is provided by the communalities. The communalities measure the proportion of each attribute's variance explained by the factor set. They are listed to the right of the factors in Table 3. Ideally, one would like to see the communalities all near 1. In the six factor solution, most of the communalities are reasonably close to 1, although a few are somewhat smaller.

Now that the descriptive data have been reduced to a set of six factors, it is possible to investigate the relationship between the descriptive attributes and overall liking, one of the key questions in this case study. This can be accomplished by performing a multiple regression of overall liking against the factor scores of the products, which can be thought of as the coordinates of the products in the six-dimensional factor space.[8]

The results of regressing overall liking against the six factors are summarized in Table 4. The regression model explained 98% of the variability in the consumer acceptance and shows that Factors 1, 2, 5, and 6 significantly affect consumer liking, as indicated by the significant t-values for those factors (see Table 4)[9]. Factor 2 is the single most influential factor, as indicated by the column titled Sum of Squares, which shows that Factor 2 accounts for more variability (or sum of squares) than the other factors. The negative sign on the parameter estimate indicates that the products with higher Factor 2 scores tend to be *less* acceptable. This is confirmed in Fig. 4, in which product acceptance (LKOVR) is plotted against Factor 2 scores. Products **d** and **k** both have high Factor 2 scores and low product acceptance, whereas

TABLE 4—*Regression model results.*

RSquare		0.980		
RSquare Adj		0.956		
Source	DF	Sum of Squares	Mean Square	F Ratio
Model	6	11.358	1.893	40.960
Error	5	0.231	0.046	Prob> F
C Total	11	11.589		0.0004
Term	Estimate	Sum of Squares	t Ratio	Prob > $\|t\|$
Intercept	4.542		73.18	0.0000
Factor 1	−0.406	1.811	−6.26	0.0015
Factor 2	−0.800	7.044	−12.35	0.0001
Factor 3	0.081	0.072	1.24	0.2685
Factor 4	−0.099	0.109	−1.53	0.1859
Factor 5	−0.437	2.098	−6.74	0.0011
Factor 6	−0.143	0.225	−2.20	0.0787

[8]A note of caution: some statistical packages may calculate factor scores inappropriately under conditions where the number of attributes entering into the factor analysis exceeds the number of products (as in this case study). Under these circumstances, it is best to consult a statistician before proceeding with any interpretation of the factor scores.

[9]With six factors and only twelve observations, there exists the risk that the data are being overfitted. Regressions with fewer factors might explain nearly as much variability as the one with six factors, and techniques such as stepwise or all possible subset regression could be employed to identify more parsimonious models.

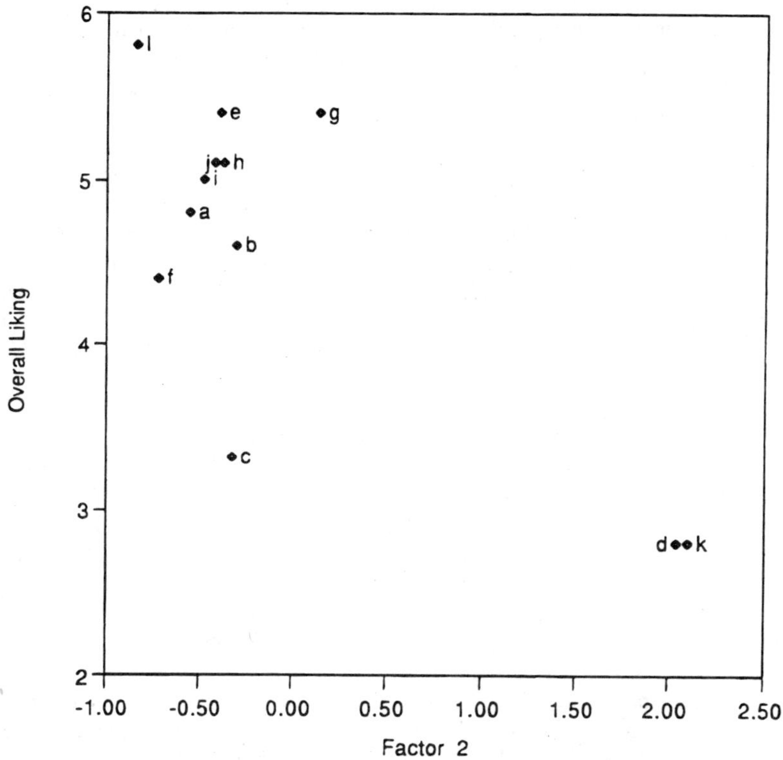

FIG. 4—*Overall liking plotted against product scores on the second factor (after rotation) of the principal component analysis.*

product **l** has a low Factor 2 score and the highest product acceptance. Since oiliness of mass (oil), cohesiveness of mass (coh2, coh3), residual chalkiness (rchalk), and lumpy appearance (vlump) have *high* positive loadings for Factor 2 (see Table 3), one can conclude that products with these attributes are *less* acceptable. By the same reasoning, attributes such as onion flavor (onion), honey aftertaste (hnaft), spreadability (sprea), level of spice complex (spice), and residual oiliness (roil), which have high *negative* Factor 2 loadings, are therefore *positively* associated with product acceptance. It is worth noting that the correlation of Factor 2 with acceptance is driven by the ratings for products **d** and **k.** Factor 2 does not distinguish among the remaining products.

Table 4 also indicates that Factor 5 is negatively related to product acceptance, but to a much lesser degree than Factor 2. The one attribute that loads highly on Factor 5 is vinegar flavor (vingr) (see Table 3), suggesting that this attribute detracts from acceptability of the salad dressings. Similar interpretations can be made of Factors 1 and 6 and their influence on overall liking.

The six-factor model seems to adequately explain the relationship between the product attributes and product acceptance. In some instances, such a model can be further refined to include curvilinear effects for some factors to better understand the relationships between the factors and product acceptance.

All of the above analyses were performed using a combination of version 6.07 of the SAS® system and JMP®[10] (Version 2.01), the SAS Institute's data visualization software for the Macintosh. Principal components analysis can be performed in many other statistical software packages available in mainframe, PC, and Macintosh environments.

2. Generalized Procrustes Analysis—Theory. Generalized Procrustes Analysis (GPA) matches two or more configurations of points (samples) in a multidimensional space by translation, scale change, rotation, and reflection [*3,4*]. The technique first derives a principal component analysis-like space for each individual data set and then "matches" these spaces through an iterative process. Some applications of this technique to sensory analysis are described by Langron [*5*], Williams and Langron [*6*], Steenkamp and van Trijp [*7*], McEwan et al. [*8*], Scriven and Mak [*9*], and Oreskovich et al. [*10*]. The method is available in several computer data analysis programs, such as SAS® [*11*] and OPP [*12*].

In this case study, the objective of the GPA was to match up as best as possible the consumer and descriptive data "spaces." The matching process uses translation, scale change, rotation, and reflection to bring these spaces into maximum alignment. At the completion of the matching process, the transformed data spaces are used to create a consensus space. The derivation of a meaningful consensus space for the consumer and descriptive panel data will allow the analyst to determine the level of agreement between the trained descriptive panelists and the consumers when evaluating similar sensory attributes, such as yellow color, sweetness, thickness, etc. The consensus space also allows the researcher to identify the descriptive attributes most related to consumer liking and to characterize the differences among the products both in descriptive and in consumer terms.

Results. GPA was applied to the descriptive panel ratings (12 products; 44 variables) and the complete set of consumer ratings (12 products; 21 variables). In a separate analysis, only the consumer liking ratings were selected for analysis with the descriptive data. The results using only liking ratings were similar to the complete analysis with respect to the relationship between liking and descriptive attributes, so only the complete analysis is discussed further. Note that in both cases GPA can safely be used even when the number of attributes exceeds the number of samples.

A statistical test of the significance of the obtained consensus has recently been devised by King and Arents [*13*]. This test determines whether there is a significant amount of agreement between the two data spaces or whether the level of agreement is no better than would be expected by chance. The GPA resulted in a highly significant consensus space, explaining 96% of the variation in the two data sets.

Similar to principal component analysis, GPA extracts a number of dimensions for the consensus configuration. The first dimension explained 80.8% of the variance in the data space, and the second dimension accounted for an additional 15.2%. The Procrustes-PC V2.0 program [*12*] employed in this analysis provides both the variable loadings and the variable correlations with the axes of the consensus space. In this study, the variable correlations rather than the variable loadings were used since the variable correlations may be interpreted statistically. The GPA output also includes factor scores for each product in the consensus space. All variable correlations and product scores can be plotted on the same graph, but with 65 variables (44 descriptive and 21 consumer variables) and 12 products such a graph is difficult to read. To simplify the presentation, three separate graphs were created. Figure 5 shows the location of the descriptive variables (plotted as vectors) in the consensus space. To minimize visual clutter, only those attributes are plotted whose correlation with the axes of

[10]Both SAS and JMP are available from SAS Institute Inc., SAS Campus Drive, Cary, NC 27513.

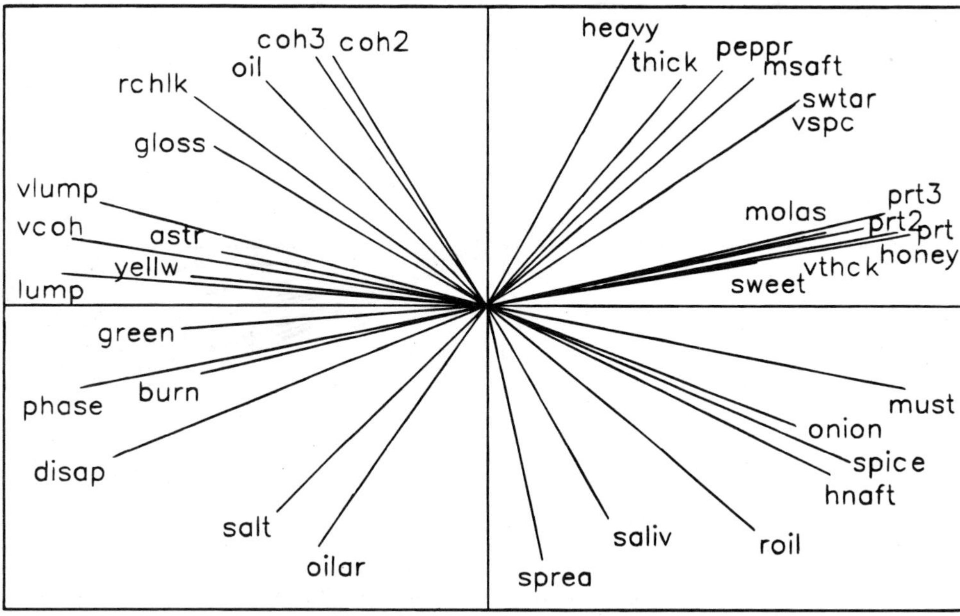

FIG. 5—*Location of the descriptive attributes in the first two dimensions of the consensus space derived by Generalized Procrustes Analysis. Only attributes with correlations greater than 0.6 are shown.*

the space was larger than approximately 0.6. Figure 6 shows the location of the consumer attributes (again, a cutoff of 0.6 was used in selecting which correlations to depict). Finally, Fig. 7 shows the positions of the products. All three figures can be overlaid to interpret the consensus space. This leads to the following conclusions regarding the key issues in this case study.

Effect of product characteristics on overall liking:

1. Overall liking (LKOVR), which falls within the range of ALL LIKING TERMS in Fig. 6, is more highly correlated with Dimension 1 (horizontal axis) than with Dimension 2 (vertical axis).
2. Figure 5 shows the descriptive attributes positively correlated with Dimension 1 and therefore positively related to overall liking (LKOVR). They include mustard flavor (must), onion/garlic flavor (onion), spice complex (spice), and honey aftertaste (hnaft). Increased perceived intensities of these attributes are associated with increased overall liking scores.
3. Descriptive attributes negatively correlated with Dimension 1 and therefore negatively related to overall liking (LKOVR) include appearance and textural lumpiness (vlump, lump) and visual cohesiveness (vcoh). Increased perceived intensities of these attributes are associated with decreased overall liking scores.

Similarities between descriptive and consumer nomenclature:

By overlaying Figs. 5 and 6, it is possible to determine the correspondence between consumer and descriptive attributes. Attributes that are located in the same region of the map are positively

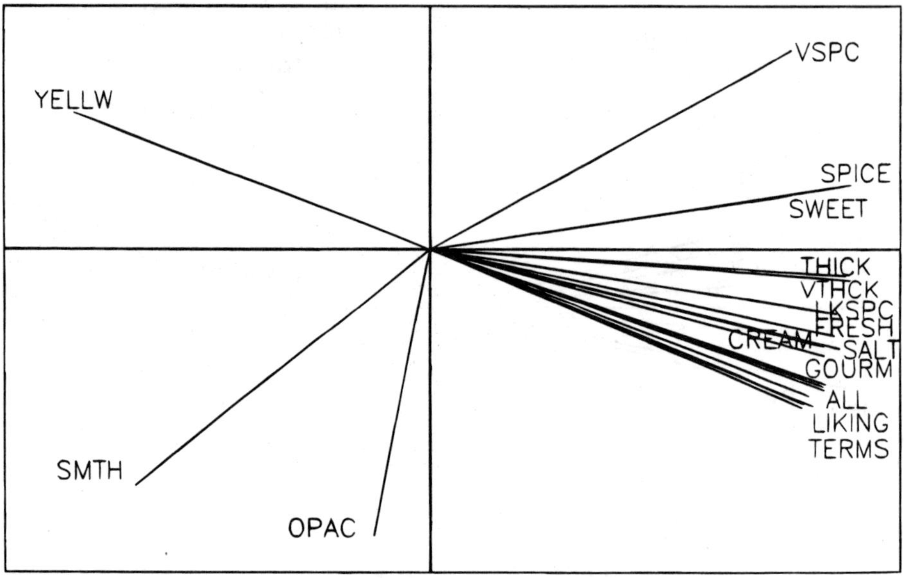

FIG. 6—*Location of the consumer attributes in the first two dimensions of the consensus space derived by Generalized Procrustes Analysis. Only attributes with correlations greater than 0.6 are shown.*

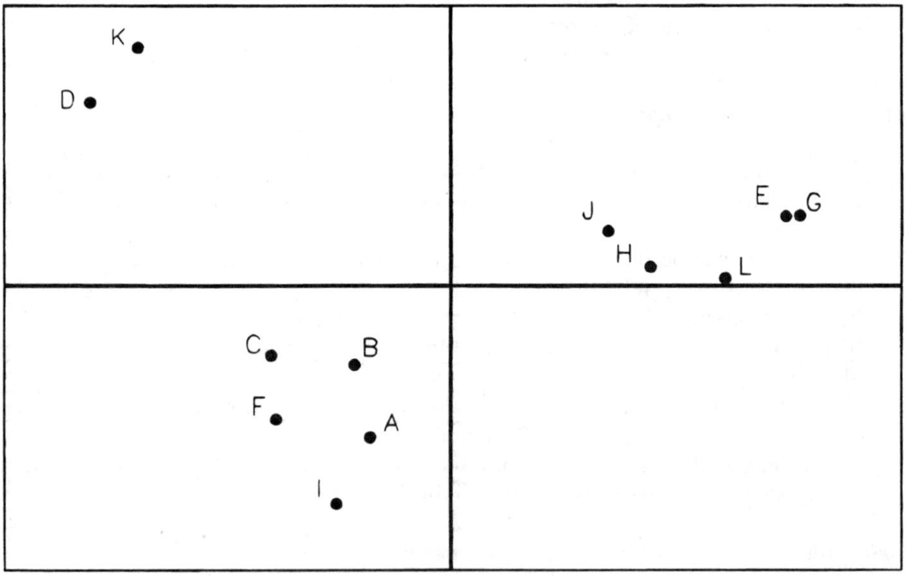

FIG. 7—*Location of the products in the first two dimensions of the consensus space derived by Generalized Procrustes Analysis.*

correlated, whereas those pointing in opposite directions from one another are negatively correlated; those perpendicular to one another are uncorrelated. The following observations result from comparing Figs. 5 and 6:

1. Consumer and descriptive variables that seem to be positively correlated are yellow (YELLW: yellw), opacity (OPAC: opac), visual thickness (VTHCK: vthck), amount of spice (VSPC: vspc, prt2, prt3, prtv), sweetness (SWEET: sweet, molas), and thickness (THICK: thick). These results suggest that the two panels agree the most when the attributes in question are easily understood by consumers, as in the case of appearance attributes or with other familiar attributes such as sweetness or thickness.
2. Other consumer and descriptive variables that seem to be related are honey-mustard flavors (HNYMS: hnaft: must). However, HNYMS is not well correlated with mustard aftertaste (msaft) nor is consumer spice intensity (SPICE) well correlated with descriptive spice flavor (spice).
3. Some variables like saltiness (SALT: salt) are inversely correlated, which is not what would be expected. This may be because consumers and descriptive judges have different concepts underlying these terms and thus score them differently. This dichotomy in scoring is also evident with consumer smoothness (SMTH) versus descriptive lumpiness (vlump, lump).

These conclusions are similar in some cases to those that one might reach based on bivariate correlations of the attributes. However, GPA displays these correlations graphically, aiding visualization, and can uncover patterns in the data that do not emerge from a mere bivariate analysis.

3. Partial Least Squares Regression—Theory. Partial least squares (PLS) regression is a relatively new approach to multivariate data analysis, which has been widely applied in chemometrics [*14*]. Applications to sensory analysis are described by Martens and Martens [*15*], Schiffman [*16*], Popper et al. [*17*], and Muñoz and Chambers [*18*]. PLS regression is used to relate a set of independent variables (e.g., descriptive panel ratings) to a set of dependent variables (e.g., consumer hedonic and attribute ratings) and can be thought of as a combination of principal component analysis and multiple regression. The algorithm underlying PLS first reduces the independent variables to a series of factors and then uses the factor scores as regressors against the dependent variables. However, unlike the approach described in the section on principal component/factor analysis, PLS performs these steps sequentially through an iterative algorithm, using the information in the dependent variables as a guide in extracting the maximally predictive factors in the independent variables.

The output of a PLS analysis includes factor loadings for the variables, factor scores for the samples, and several measures of how well the dependent variables are predicted by the independent variables. The benefits of PLS compared to other methods are discussed by Martens and Van der Burg [*19*] and Martens and Martens [*15*]. PLS is well suited for sensory analysis for several reasons [*15*]. PLS regression is well-equipped to handle large numbers of attributes and can be performed even when the number of attributes exceeds the number of samples and when there is a high degree of correlation (multicollinearity) within the independent or dependent variables. Partial least squares regression is included in several computer programs for data analysis, such as The Unscrambler™ [*20*] and Pirouette™ [*21*].

Results. PLS was applied to the present case study to discover which appearance, flavor, and texture attributes rated by the descriptive panel were correlated with consumer liking. PLS was also used to assess the agreement between trained panelists and consumers on the use of similar sensory attributes, such as sweetness, thickness, etc. All 44 descriptive attributes were used as independent (predictor) variables. All 21 consumer ratings, including both hedonic and intensity ratings, were used as dependent variables to be predicted by the 44 descriptive attributes. The effect of limiting the dependent variables to overall liking (excluding the consumer intensity ratings and other hedonics) was also investigated. Both approaches gave similar results with respect to overall liking and its relationship to the descriptive attributes. Therefore, only the larger analysis that includes all the consumer data is reported here.

All variables, descriptive as well as consumer, were first standardized to zero mean and unit variance to eliminate differences in scale types. The data were then submitted to PLS analysis using the Unscrambler program. Similar to a principal component analysis, PLS regression results in the extraction of a number of factors. In the present study, the analysis indicated that the first two PLS factors accounted for only 62% of variability in the descriptive data, suggesting the need for additional factors to explain a greater amount of the variation in the data. However, the primary objective of PLS regression was to extract factors that would maximally predict the consumer, not the descriptive data. The same two PLS factors were found to account for 86% of the variability in the consumer data, which was considered excellent.

The output of the PLS regression includes factor loadings for every variable (consumer and descriptive) as well as factor scores for each of the samples. Since the results of the PLS regression are similar to those of the Procrustes Analysis (see next section for a direct comparison), only some of the results will be shown here.

Figure 8 shows the loadings on the first two PLS factors for overall liking and several consumer (capital letters) and descriptive attributes whose loadings were "large" (roughly the

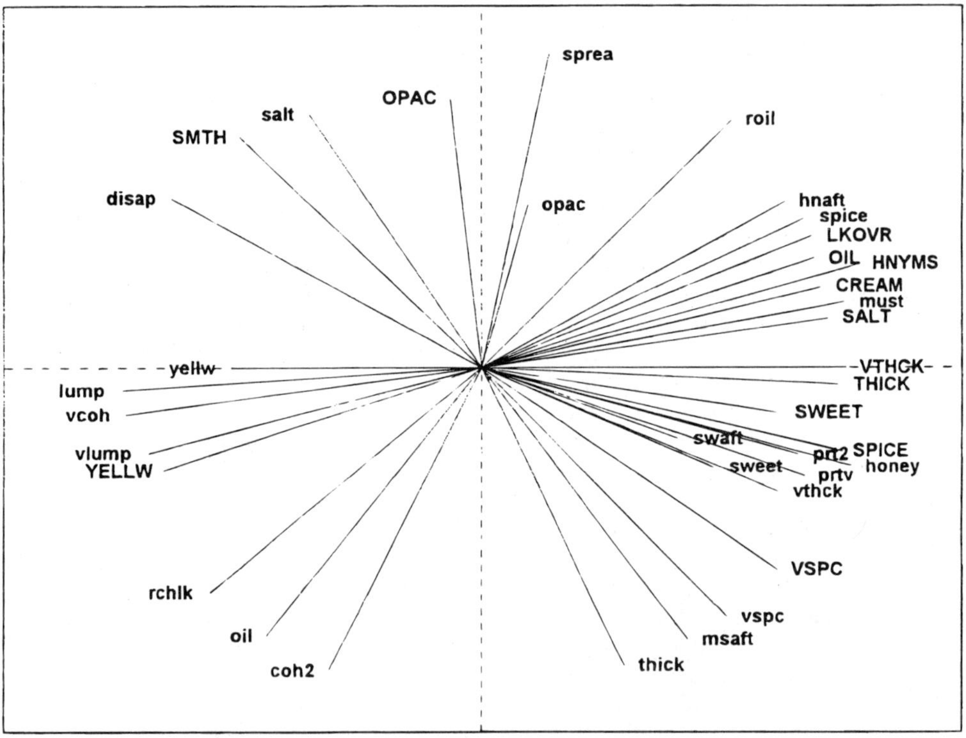

FIG. 8—*Loadings of the descriptive (lowercase) and consumer (upper case) attributes on the first two factors of the partial least squares analysis. Not all attributes are shown.*

same magnitude as the loading for overall liking). Several facts emerge from a consideration of Fig. 8:

1. Overall liking (LKOVR) is much more highly correlated with Factor 1 (horizontal axis) than with Factor 2 (vertical axis).
2. The descriptive attributes positively correlated with Factor 1 and therefore positively related to overall liking include honey aftertaste (hnaft), spice complex (spice), and mustard flavor (must). Higher levels of these attributes are associated with higher levels of overall liking.
3. The descriptive attributes negatively correlated with Factor 1 and therefore negatively related to overall liking include lumpy appearance (vlump), lumpy texture (lump), and cohesive appearance (vcoh). Higher levels of these attributes are associated with decreases in overall liking.
4. Consumers' ratings of saltiness (SALT) are unrelated (or at least not linearly related) to the descriptive ratings of the same attribute (salt). Since consumer ratings of saltiness were correlated with overall liking, consideration of only the consumer data would have suggested that increasing saltiness will increase consumer acceptability. The data, however, show that increasing the amount of salt in the product is unlikely to improve its acceptability (assuming that the descriptive ratings accurately track the amount of sodium in the product).
5. Creaminess (CREAM), for the consumer, can be related to several descriptive appearance and texture attributes. Creaminess is negatively correlated with lumpy appearance (vlump), cohesive appearance (vcoh), cohesive texture (coh2), and residual chalkiness (rchlk), but is positively related to the amount of oily residue (roil). The correlation with honey aftertaste (hnaft) may be incidental. Taken together, these results suggest how one would formulate a salad dressing that is perceived as particularly "creamy" by consumers.
6. Smoothness (SMTH), for consumers, is strongly positively related to rate of disappearance (disap) and, to a lesser extent, negatively related to visual and textural thickness (vthick, thick). Smoothness and creaminess, both consumer terms, are unrelated to one another.

In the addition to variable loadings, PLS provides information on the samples in the form of factor scores (not shown here). Other useful output includes an assessment of the degree to which the two PLS factors explain individual consumer variables such as overall liking, creaminess, etc. It was reported above that overall 86% of the total variation in the consumer data was explained by the first two PLS factors; however, this leaves open the possibility that some individual variables are less well explained than others. In this case study, almost all consumer variables were explained equally well (>75% variance accounted for), but in other cases the analysis might identify certain consumer terms for which there are no descriptive correlates, suggesting areas where additional terminology might be developed.

IV. Comparisons Among the Methods and Conclusions

It is possible to make a direct comparison between the Procrustes and PLS analyses because the approaches lead to very similar types of output, namely factor scores for the samples and variable loadings or correlations for the attributes. The results of the Procrustes and PLS analyses were compared by correlating the variable loadings obtained in PLS with the variable correlations obtained in Procrustes for the 65 attributes in the study. The correlation between the first PLS and first Procrustes dimension was 0.99, between the second dimensions −0.79, indicating a very similar placement of the variables in two-dimensional space. The similarity is also apparent when comparing the positions of those attributes common to Figs. 5, 6, and 8. Note that the second PLS dimension is simply reversed in direction compared to the second Procrustes dimension. The PLS and Procrustes *scores* for the twelve salad dressings were also correlated, resulting in correlations of 0.99 between the first dimensions and 0.98 between the second dimensions. A plot of the sample scores for PLS (not shown) reveals a very similar pattern to that displayed in Fig. 7 for the Procrustes consensus space. The fact that PLS regression and Procrustes yield similar results is reassuring, given that they use the same data and have the common objective of relating one data "space" to another, albeit by different means.

To compare the results of all three multivariate approaches, as well as the simple bivariate correlation approach, a more intuitive, less statistically based approach can be taken. Table 5 compares the methods in terms of the descriptive attributes found to be important to overall liking. Those attributes are identified by a + or −, depending on whether the correlation with overall liking is positive or negative.

The differences in the results reflect both the inherent differences among the methods as well as the judgment invariably involved in selecting those variables most important to overall liking. Nonetheless, it is clear that there are a number of similarities. All methods identify the level of spice complex, mustard flavor, and honey aftertaste as positively related to overall liking. All methods, except principal component regression, identify lumpy and cohesive appearance and lumpy texture as negatively related to overall liking (the principal component regression also identifies them as negatively related, but gives them slightly less importance relative to other attributes). Note that simple bivariate correlations are as effective as multivariate methods in identifying these attributes as important to overall liking. However, the bivariate methods do not provide as rich an understanding of the numerous and complex interrelationships among the descriptive and consumer data as do the three multivariate approaches.

TABLE 5—*Descriptive attributes correlated with consumers acceptance by method of analysis.*

Attribute	Bivariate Correlations	Principal Component Regression	Generalized Procrustes Analysis	Partial Least Squares Regression
Lumpy appearance (vlump)	−	−	−	−
Cohes. appearance (vcoh)	−	...	−	−
Phase separation (phase)	...	...	...	...
Spice complex (spice)	+	+	+	+
Mustard flavor (must)	+	+	+	+
Onion flavor (onion)	+	...	+	+
Honey aftertaste (hnaft)	+	+	+	+
Lumpiness (lump)	−	...	−	−
Oiliness of mass (oil)	...	−	...	...
Cohesiveness of mass	...	−	...	...
Residual oiliness (roil)	+	+	...	...
Residual chalkiness (rchalk)	−	−	...	...

NOTE: The symbols + or − indicate a positive or negative correlation with overall liking.

APPENDIX 1

TABLE A1—*Descriptive attributes.**

Full Name	Abbreviation
APPEARANCE	
lumpiness (visual)	vlump
thickness (visual)	vthck
cohesiveness (flow) (visual)	vcoh
amount of spice particles (visual)	vspc
product (phase) separation	phase
yellow color	yellw
opacity	opac
gloss	gloss
FLAVOR	
spice complex	spice
mustard	must
green complex	green
black pepper	peppr
overall sweet aromatics	swtar
honey	honey
molasses	molas
caramelized	carml
onion/garlic	onion
oil aromatic	oilar
vinegar	vingr
saltiness	salt
sweetness	sweet
sourness	sour
burn	burn
astringency	astr
honey aftertaste	hnaft
mustard aftertaste	msaft
salty aftertaste	slaft
sweet aftertaste	swaft
sour aftertaste	sraft
TEXTURE	
heaviness	heavy
thickness	thick
spreadability	sprea
lumpy	lump
cohesiveness of mass (stage 2**)	coh2
amount of spice particles (stage 2)	prt2
particle size variability	prtv
oiliness of mass	oil
amount of spice particles (stage 3)	prt3
cohesiveness of mass (stage 3)	coh3
rate of disappearance	disap
saliva production (residual)	saliv
chemical burn (residual)	rburn
oily (residual)	roil
chalky (residual)	rchlk

*All attributes were measured on unstructured line scales representing intensity.
**Stages 2 and 3 refer to time points during mastication.

TABLE A2—*Consumer attributes.**

Full Name	Abbreviation
appetizing (visual)	VAPPT
opacity	OPAC
amount spice (visual)	VSPC
thickness (visual)	VTHCK
yellow	YELLW
fresh flavor	FRESH
creamy flavor	CREAM
gourmet flavor	GOURM
overall spice/herb flavor	SPICE
honey/mustard flavor	HNYMS
thickness	THICK
saltiness	SALT
sweetness	SWEET
oily	OIL
smoothness	SMTH
liking of appearance	LKAPP
liking of taste/flavor	LKFLV
liking of spice/herb combination	LKSPC
liking of honey mustard flavor	LKHNM
liking of texture	LKTEX
overall liking	LKOVR

*All attributes were measured on either 9-point hedonic scales (in the case of the last six attributes) or 9-point intensity scales (in the case of all the other attributes).

References

[*1*] Jackson, J. E., *A User's Guide to Principal Components,* Wiley, New York, 1991.

[2] Gabriel, K. R., "The Biplot Graphic Display of Matrices with Application to Principal Component Analysis," *Biometrika,* Vol. 58, No. 3, 1971, pp. 453–467.

[*3*] Gower, J. C., "Generalized Procrustes Analysis," *Psychometrika,* Vol. 40, 1975, pp. 33–51.

[*4*] Dijksterhuis, G. and Punter, P., "Interpreting Generalized Procrustes Analysis 'Analysis of Variance' Tables," *Food Quality and Preference,* Vol. 2, 1990, pp. 255–265.

[*5*] Langron, S. P., "The Application of Procrustes Statistics to Sensory Profiling," in *Sensory Quality in Foods and Beverages: Definition, Measurement, and Control,* A. A. Williams and R. K. Atkin, Eds., Ellis Horwood Ltd., Chichester, U.K., 1983, pp. 89–95.

[*6*] Williams, A. A. and Langron, S. P., "The Use of Free Choice Profiling for the Examination of Commercial Ports," *Journal of Science, Food, and Agriculture,* Vol. 35, 1984, pp. 558–568.

[*7*] Steenkamp, J.-B. E. M. and van Trijp, H. C. M., "Free Choice Profiling in Cognitive Food Acceptance Research," in *Food Acceptability,* D. M. H. Thompson, Ed., Elsevier Applied Science, London, U.K., 1988, pp. 363–376.

[*8*] McEwan, J. A., Colwill, J. S., and Thomson, D. M. H., "The Application of Two Free-Choice Profiling Methods to Investigate the Sensory Characteristics of Chocolate," *Journal of Sensory Studies,* Vol. 3, 1989, pp. 271–286.

[9] Scriven, F. M. and Mak, Y. L., "Usage Behavior of Meat Products by Australians and Hong Kong Chinese: A Comparison of Free Choice and Consensus Profiling," *Journal of Sensory Studies,* Vol. 6, 1991, pp. 25–36.

[*10*] Oreskovich, D. C., Klein, B. P., and Sutherland, J. W., "Procrustes Analysis and Its Applications to Free-Choice and Other Sensory Profiling," in *Sensory Science: Theory and Applications in Foods,* T. H. Lawless and B. P. Klein, Eds., Marcel Dekker Inc., New York, 1991.

[*11*] Schlich, P., A SAS/IML Program for Generalized Procrustes Analysis. SEUGI '89, *Proceedings of the SAS European Users Group International Conference,* 9–12 May 1989, Cologne, 1989, SAS Institute, Inc., Cary, NC, pp. 529–537.

[*12*] OPP, 1992. Oliemans, Punter and Partners: Procrustes V2.0. Utrecht, The Netherlands.

[*13*] King, B. M. and Arents, P., "A Statistical Test of Consensus Obtained from Generalized Procrustes Analysis of Sensory Data, *Journal of Sensory Studies,* Vol. 6, 1991, pp. 37–48.

[14] Geladi, P. and Kowalski, B. R., "Partial Least-Squares Regression: A Tutorial," *Analytica Chimica Acta,* Vol. 185, 1986, pp. 1–17.
[15] Martens, M. and Martens, H., "Partial Least Squares Regression," in *Statistical Procedures in Food Research,* J. R. Piggott, Ed., Elsevier, London, 1986, pp. 293–359.
[16] Schiffman, S., "Basic Concepts of Multidimensional Scaling," in *Applied Sensory Analysis of Foods,* Vol. 2, H. Moskowitz, Ed., CRC Press, Boca Raton, 1988, pp. 3–33.
[17] Popper, R., Risvik, E., Martens, H., and Martens, M., "A Comparison of Multivariate Approaches to Sensory Analysis and the Prediction of Acceptability," in *Food Acceptability,* D. M. H. Thomson, Ed., Elsevier, London, 1988, pp. 401–410.
[18] Muñoz, A. M. and Chambers, E., "Relating Sensory Measurements to Consumer Acceptance of Meat Products," *Food Technology,* 1993, pp. 128–134.
[19] Martens, M. and Van der Burg, E., "Relating Sensory and Instrumental Data from Vegetables Using Different Multivariate Techniques," in *Progress in Flavor Research,* J. Adda, Ed., Elsevier, Amsterdam, pp. 131–148.
[20] The Unscrambler, 1993. CAMO, Trondheim, Norway.
[21] Pirouette, 1991. Infometrix, Inc., Seattle.

by Lori Rothman[1]

Chapter 6—Relationship Between Consumer Responses and Analytical Measurements

I. Problem/Objective

A. To determine the relationships between analytical measurements and consumer responses for herb and cheese breadsticks.

B. To predict consumer responses based on analytical measurements.

II. Approach

A. Tests

The analytical tests included moisture (%), fat (%), protein (%), Hunter *l, a, b,* Instron load (kg) and Instron slope (kg/cm).

Consumer response data from 126 respondents for eight samples included overall, appearance, flavor, and texture liking (9-point hedonic category scales where 9 = like extremely, 1 = dislike extremely) and "just right" evaluations for color, cheese, salt, and hardness (7-point category scales where 7 = much too ________, 4 = just right, and 1 = not nearly ________ enough). Average scores for all consumer and instrumental attributes are given in Table 1.

B. Test Design

One batch of each of the eight bread sticks was produced and split for analytical and consumer evaluations, which were conducted during the same week (four weeks after production). Samples were exposed to similar environmental conditions throughout the study.

III. Data Analysis

A. Summary and Theoretical Discussion

Graphical assessment and correlational analysis were used to investigate the relationships between consumer responses and analytical measures, while univariate, multivariate, and principal components regression were used to develop prediction equations for consumer responses based on instrumental measurements. Product means were used in all cases (n = 8).

1. Graphical

Graphing each analytical measure (x axis) versus each consumer response (y axis) is a simple and direct way to visualize relationships and will assist in the initial determination of

[1]Group leader, Kraft Foods, Inc., 801 Waukegan Rd., Glenview, IL 60026.

TABLE 1—*Mean scores for consumer and analytical measures.*

9-pt. Scales	501	928	472	835	293	760	316	045
Overall Liking	6.9	6.6	6.2	6.0	6.8	6.8	5.6	5.1
Appearance Liking	6.4	6.3	6.7	5.7	7.5	7.0	5.5	5.6
Flavor Liking	6.8	6.6	6.0	5.7	6.5	6.8	5.8	5.3
Texture Liking	6.5	6.5	6.0	5.7	6.2	6.3	4.8	4.4
7-pt. Scales	**501**	**928**	**472**	**835**	**293**	**760**	**316**	**045**
Color Just Right	4.0	4.3	4.3	4.5	4.1	4.5	4.8	4.3
Cheese Just Right	3.4	3.4	3.1	3.1	3.4	3.4	3.3	3.1
Salt Just Right	3.9	3.8	3.5	3.6	3.7	3.8	3.7	3.5
Hard Just Right	4.4	4.5	4.3	4.8	4.6	4.7	5.4	4.6
Analytical Measures	**501**	**928**	**472**	**835**	**293**	**760**	**316**	**045**
Moisture, %	3.81	3.84	4.77	3.90	4.66	4.17	3.55	5.11
Fat, %	16.45	16.85	15.43	16.54	16.25	16.7	15.96	15.71
Protein, %	5.46	5.65	5.77	5.70	5.52	5.51	5.43	5.34
l, Hunter	44.7	44.3	44.6	43.8	46.8	43.1	41.0	45.5
a, Hunter	17.0	17.7	17.6	17.5	15.7	15.9	15.7	16.1
b, Hunter	33.6	33.5	31.8	31.2	33.4	30.1	27.1	30.6
Load, kg	1.95	2.17	2.45	1.89	3.19	2.66	2.57	2.82
Slope, kg	57.6	49.8	69.7	60.3	87.0	82.7	73.3	62.0

whether the relationships are linear, quadratic (curved), or whether no apparent relationship exists. The detection of outliers (points that appear to be outside a given relationship) can be initially determined using graphical assessment. It is also important to visually verify that an observed relationship would still exist if any one point were removed from the graph.

2. Correlations

Determination of the correlation coefficient, *r*, for each analytical measure with each consumer response will allow assessment of the degree of linearity of the relationship. Because quadratic relationships take the form of an inverted U, the correlation coefficient cannot be used to determine the strength of these relationships. The correlation coefficient also does not provide information concerning the steepness of slope of the relationship; this is determined by the regression coefficient. One or two extreme data points can exert undue influence on *r*; that is why both graphical and correlational methods are recommended.

3. Regression—Univariate: Linear and Quadratic

Univariate, (one variable) regression may be used to develop a prediction equation to relate two variables when one variable has a moderate to high correlation with another. The R^2 (variation in y explained by x as a decimal) will be the square of the correlation coefficient. The probability of the F value associated with the equation is the probability that if the slope were 0, a regression coefficient of the magnitude observed would result by chance. The plot of residuals (the observed value of y minus the value of y predicted by the equation) (y axis) versus the predicted value of y (x axis) should show a random distribution of points. A non-random distribution means that errors associated with poor fit of the regression may be due to a systematic effect, such as lack of a higher order (squared) term or a need to transform the data prior to generating an equation.

When graphical evaluation reveals a curved relationship or when a linear equation inadequately models the relationship, regression using a quadratic term may be appropriate. Both the linear and squared terms are part of the regression equation, which is still considered univariate. The quadratic term defines the curvature, which may denote an optimal value of the dependent liking variable within the sample set; the linear term orients the curve.

4. Regression—Multivariate

Multiple regression will yield equations with more than one independent variable that together explain variation in the dependent variables. These equations are based on linear models. Prior to running analyses, the data must be examined for multicollinearity, or intercorrelation of the dependent variables. If dependent variables are highly correlated, the equations developed have unstable parameter estimates (slope and intercept) and their standard errors are inflated [*1*]. Determining the importance of a given predictor is difficult because the effects of the predictors are confounded [*1*]. The degree of collinearity affects the quality of the predicted values of the response variable, inflating the variances of predicted values for independent variable values not included in the original sample. However, statisticians do not agree on the magnitude of correlation between two predictor variables that may lead to erroneous findings.

For developing prediction equations it has been suggested that if the correlation between two predictor variables is greater than that between either predictor variable and the dependent variable, one of the independent variables should be eliminated. It is advisable to leave each independent variable out of the equation, in turn, to examine the difference in the final equation. Another strategy is to develop a new variable that incorporates two correlated independent variables, such as their ratio or sum.

There are caveats particular to the use of regression analysis with "just right" scales as a technique for understanding data relationships. These scales may not be normally distributed; other analyses that do not assume normality may be more appropriate. However, the sample means become normally distributed very quickly as sample size increases. Thus, results should be fairly correct, no matter how the scores were actually distributed. The widespread use of these scales (and this type of analysis) coupled with the lack of agreement about which analyses are appropriate has led to their inclusion here.

a. All Subsets

All possible subsets is a method for generating regression equations with 1 to n independent variables, where n is the number of degrees of freedom available (generally the number of data points minus two because the intercept takes up one degree of freedom). The candidate models are evaluated by the experimenter using any or all of the following criteria: maximizing R^2 (variance in y explained by x), maximizing adjusted R^2 (variance explained accounting for the number of terms in the model; adding a term to the model will always increase R^2, while a corresponding decrease in adjusted R^2 indicates that the model may be overfit), optimizing Mallow's C_p [2] (to approximate the number of terms in the model, including the intercept), minimizing the PRESS Statistic [*2*] (omit each observation in turn, fit a model to the remaining data, predict the missing data points, and square the discrepancies; compare the sum of squares of these discrepancies for all candidate models), and minimizing the mean square error (average variance of the observations from the predicted observations). If data sets are very large, this method may be costly in terms of computer resources.

Equations should be examined and adjusted for multicollinearity between the independent variables and for the significance of each term in the equation (except the intercept, whose significance is often of little concern). Statisticians disagree as to the significance level required for inclusion of a given term in the model.

In general, the fewer independent variables included in the model that achieve the objective, the better.

b. Stepwise Regression

An alternate and commonly used method for developing regression equations is the stepwise procedure, whereby variables are entered and deleted from the model based on their significance level with other terms already in the model. The first variable entered is the one with the highest correlation with the dependent variable. This means that if two variables, *a* and *b*, together explain more variation than a third variable, *c*, does alone, stepwise may not determine the equation with variables *a* and *b;* it may only determine the equation with variable *c*. This is one important drawback to stepwise regression.

c. Principal Component Regression

The issue of intercorrelation of independent variables was discussed earlier. In data sets where this is a problem, removal of this intercorrelation would allow a more straightforward generation of equations. Principal components analysis groups together correlated variables into principal components, which are orthogonal (uncorrelated) to one another. These principal components can then be treated as independent variables to predict dependent variable response. Because principal components analysis groups together highly related variables, it may be possible to account for much of the variation explained by all the independent variables in only two or three principal components, thereby simplifying the data. After the components are extracted, a process called rotation may be used for ease of interpretation. Rotation does not change the total amount of variation explained or the final communality estimates, the variation explained in individual variables accounted for by the components. It does, however, change the amount of variation explained by each principal component.

In general, with varimax rotation [*3*], each factor tends to load highly on a few variables and lower on other variables, making interpretation of resulting factors easier than when other rotation methods are used [*1*].

One final comment relating to both univariate and multivariate regression methods: you cannot be sure that your model is truly predictive without some means of validation. For large data sets, this can be approximated using subsets of the original data; for small data sets, such as the one presented here, validation would be accomplished using a new data set.

B. Results

1. Graphical

Table 2 lists relationships apparent from visual analysis.

a. Linear/Correlational

Fat appears linearly related to overall liking, flavor liking, texture liking, and cheese "just right"; *b* appears linearly related to overall liking (Fig. 1), flavor liking, and color "just right"; moisture appears linearly related to salt "just right."

TABLE 2—*Consumer/instrumental relationships evident from graphical analysis.*

	Overall	Appearance	Flavor	Texture	Size	Color	Cheese	Salt	Hard
Moisture	Q	Q**	Q	Q	...	...	...	L**	...
Fat	L	...	L	L*	...	...	L	...	...
Protein	...	Q	Q	...	...	...	Q	...	...
l	...	...	...	...	...	L	...	...	...
a	...	...	Q**	...	...	...	...	...	...
b	L	...	L**	...	...	L	...	...	...
Load	...	...	...	...	...	...	...	...	...
Slope	...	...	...	...	...	...	...	...	...

NOTE:
L = Linear.
Q = Quadritic.
L* = presence of an outlier.
L**, Q** = Illogical relationship.

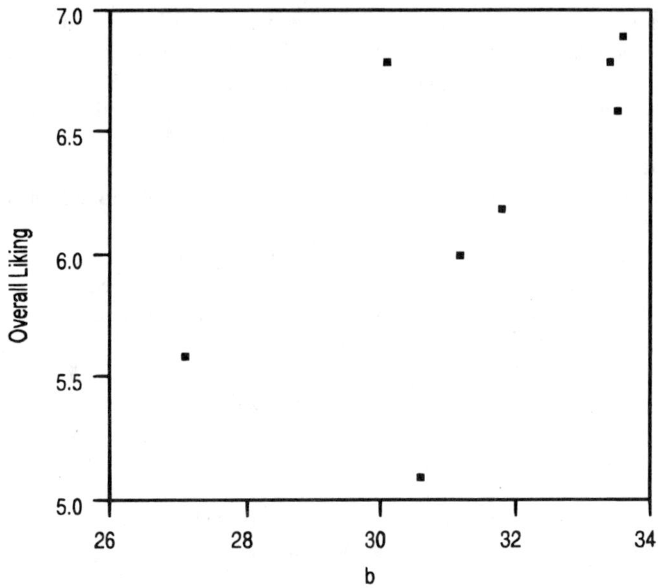

FIG. 1—*Example of a linear relationship.*

Before proceeding further, the data should be examined to make sure the relationships make logical sense. It is doubtful that *b* (loosely defined as "green") relates to flavor liking per se, but probably to other variables that in turn relate to flavor liking. It is also doubtful that moisture level would relate to appropriateness of salt level within the tested range.

Notice also that although it was not apparent visually, there are strong linear relationships between fat and salt "just right," texture liking and *b,* and hard "just right," with *l* and *b* (Table 3). This reinforces the point that both graphical and correlational analyses are helpful in looking for data relationships. Again, these relationships should be examined logically before proceeding.

b. Quadratic

The relationship between moisture and overall liking (Fig. 2) falls into this category, with moistures between 4 and 4.65% optimal. Seven other relationships (Table 2) display similar patterns. As with the linear relationships, the logical nature of these relationships should be considered before proceeding further.

TABLE 3—*Correlations of independent variables with consumer responses.*

	Moisture	Fat	Protein	*l*	*a*	*b*	Load	Slope
Overall Liking	−0.28	0.60	0.30	0.24	−0.16	0.63	−0.13	0.18
Appearance Liking	0.28	0.18	0.22	0.52	−0.14	0.54	0.43	0.58
Flavor Liking	−0.36	0.64	0.11	0.10	0.04	0.51	−0.09	0.15
Texture Liking	−0.27	0.59	0.51	0.25	0.42	0.71	−0.29	−0.01
Color Just Right	−0.39	−0.06	−0.02	−0.86	−0.24	−0.91	−0.02	0.15
Cheese Just Right	−0.45	0.65	−0.26	0.03	−0.30	0.27	0.12	0.22
Salt Just Right	−0.67	0.76	−0.20	−0.17	−0.07	0.28	−0.27	−0.06
Hard Just Right	−0.50	0.02	−0.37	−0.74	−0.54	−0.84	0.12	0.25

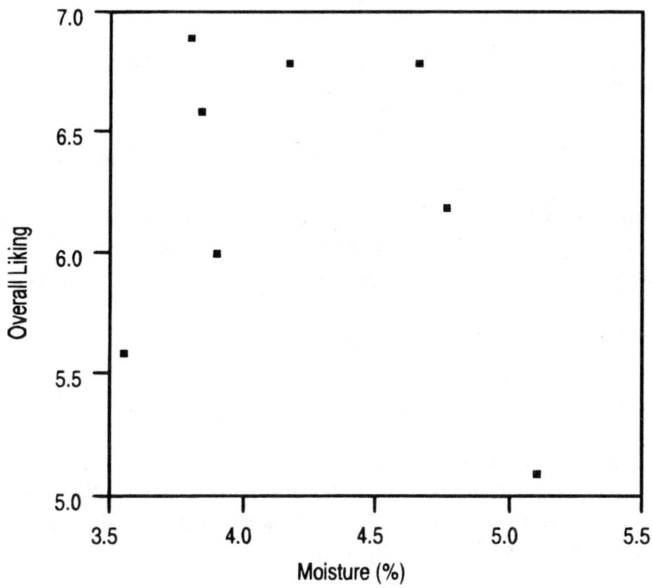

FIG. 2—*Example of a quadratic relationship.*

c. No Relationship

Figure 3 gives an example of a relationship with no apparent linear or quadratic pattern; these relationships are represented by the dashed lines in Table 2.

2. Univariate Regression

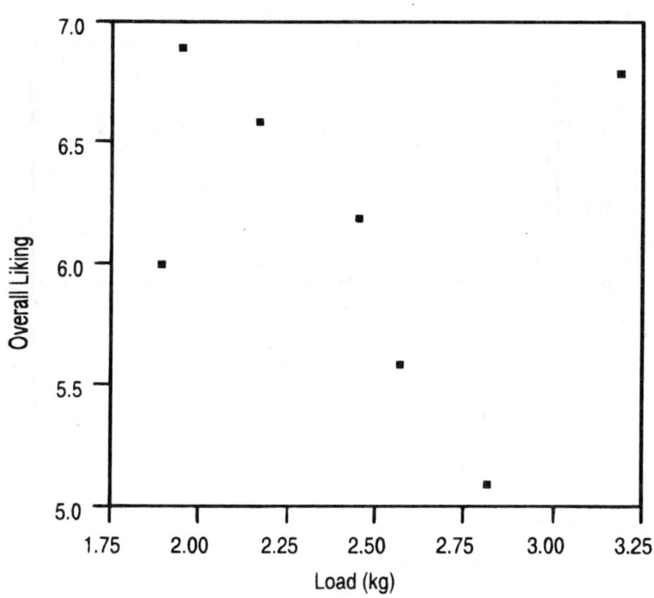

FIG. 3—*Example of no relationship.*

a. Linear

Linear relationships were developed for the seven "logical" relationships in Table 2. Three will be discussed. The equation to relate overall liking to *b* is:

$$\text{overall liking} = 0.479679 + 0.183695(b), \text{ with } R^2 = 0.39, \text{ and prob}(F) = 0.10$$

This equation has too low an R^2 to be of any predictive value; the prob(F) is also considered borderline (the slope may still be 0). The plot of residuals versus predicted values is given in Fig. 4. Notice the random distribution of points, indicating that a linear model may be the best fit.

The equation to relate *b* to color "just right" is:

$$\text{color "just right"} = 7.572030 - 0.102572(b), \text{ with } R^2 = 0.82 \text{ and prob}(F)\ 0.002$$

As *b* increases, the product is perceived as closer to "just right" in color; as *b* decreases, the product is perceived as "too dark." As shown in Table 1, the range of "just right" color scores is from 4.0 (just right) to 4.8 (slightly too dark). This equation can be used for prediction.

The equation to relate texture liking with fat is:

$$\text{texture liking} = -9.544547 + 0.945080(\text{fat}) \text{ with } R^2 = 0.35 \text{ and prob}(F) = 0.12$$

This equation is not significant, indicating a non-predictive linear relationship. However, re-examination of the relationship between texture liking and fat (Fig. 5) reveals the presence of an outlier (Product 472). If this product is excluded from analysis the equation is:

$$\text{texture liking} = -24.317842 + 1.840162(\text{fat}) \text{ with } R^2 = 0.77, \text{ and prob}(F) = 0.009$$

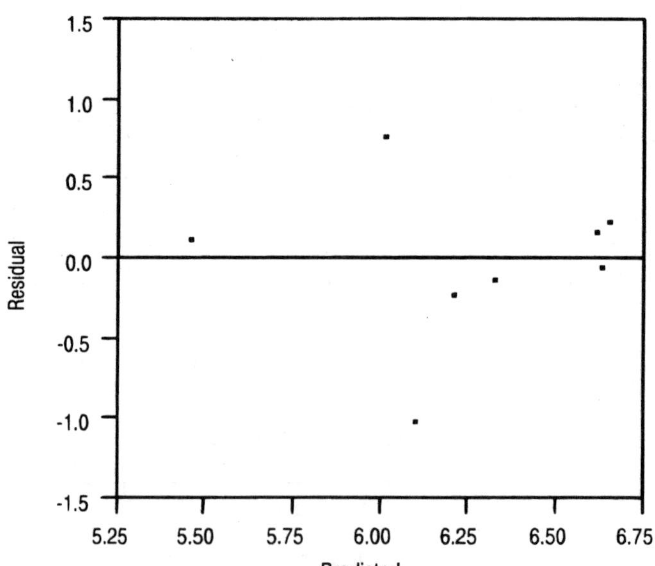

FIG. 4—*Plot of residuals versus predicted values for overall liking versus* b.

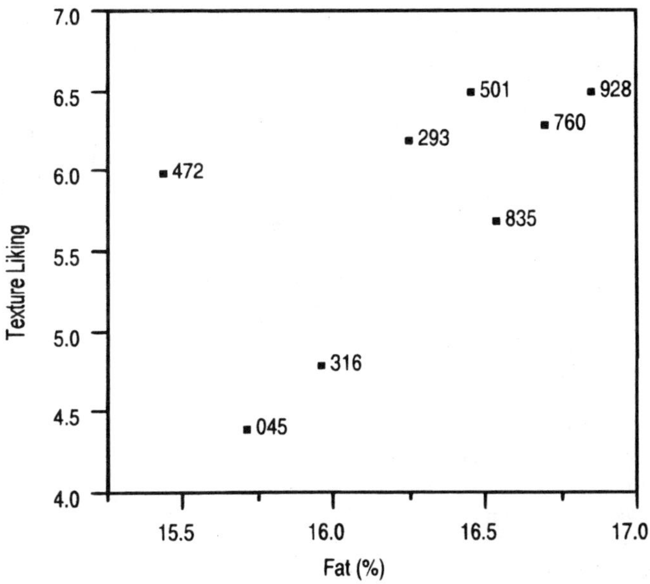

FIG. 5—*Example of one product not following the relationship.*

It is important to examine reasons for the "outlier" status, including sample production error, measurement error, dissimilarity of this sample to others, etc. The decision to exclude an outlier should be a joint recommendation from all parties involved in the study.

b. Quadratic

As discussed earlier, there was a curved relationship between overall liking and moisture. The quadratic equation is:

$$\text{overall liking} = -38.216292 + 21.65242(\text{moisture}) - 2.48109(\text{moisture}^2)$$
$$\text{with } R^2 = 0.76 \text{ and prob}(F) = 0.003$$

Both the linear and quadratic terms are significant ($p = 0.01, 0.01$). More than half the variation in overall liking is accounted for by the moisture terms. This equation can be used for prediction.

Significant relationships were developed for three other relationships listed in Table 2; only one other will be discussed:

$$\text{texture liking} = -50.191809 + 26.618773(\text{moisture}) - 3.116621(\text{moisture}^2)$$
$$\text{with } R^2 = 0.80, \text{ and prob}(F) = 0.02$$

This equation relates moisture content to texture liking, yields an optimal moisture range, and explains the majority of variation in liking scores. As seen earlier, moisture content was also related to overall liking; one could postulate that this is due to the effect moisture has on texture.

3. Multivariate Regression

a. All Subsets

For this data set, many of the analytical variables exhibited moderate (0.6) to strong (0.8) correlations with one another (Table 4) that were greater than their correlations with the consumer measure of interest. It was therefore necessary to run a series of multiple regressions for each consumer response variable, eliminating models that contained variables highly correlated to others in the equation. Because there were eight products in this study and one degree of freedom is required for the intercept, only six analytical variables at one time could be considered for all subsets regression (2).

To allow for curvature in the models, squared terms of all the variables should also be included. This would increase the number of independent variables from 8 to 16. Sixteen variables taken six at a time (the maximum number allowed to be considered in all subsets regression where $n = 8$) results in 8008 possible combinations of variables for the computer to examine. If one additionally included interaction (cross product) terms, the number of variables to be considered increases dramatically. It is for this reason that only linear terms were included, with the understanding that this could limit the usefulness of the prediction equations. Because of the small number of products, it was additionally decided to limit models to those with three or fewer variables.

After careful consideration of all candidate models for predicting overall liking, the model with the highest adjusted R^2 with three variables was examined further.

$$\text{overall liking} = 7.337439 + 0.527684(b) - 0.458024(l) + 0.03824\,(\text{slope})$$
$$\text{with } R^2 = 0.97,\ \text{adjusted } R^2 = 0.95 \text{ and prob}(F) = 0.0012$$

All parameter estimates are significant at $p < 0.01$. However, this model has two highly correlated variables (Table 4), l and b. Each of these variables has a positive correlation with overall liking (Table 3), yet the sign of the coefficient for l in the equation is negative when b is in the equation. In other words, with b in the equation, l now has a negative effect on overall liking. In fact, l and b are more highly correlated with each other than either is with overall liking. This and the reversal of the sign of one of the coefficients leads to a rejection of this model.

The model with the next highest adjusted R^2 was:

$$\text{overall liking} = 1.395965 + 0.275041(b) - 0.749462(\text{moisture})$$
$$+ 0.03206(\text{slope}) \text{ with } R^2 = 0.88,\ \text{adjusted } R^2 = 0.80 \text{ and prob}(F) = 0.02$$

All parameter estimates are significant at $p < 0.05$. None of the three independent variables were highly correlated with each other, so multicollinearity is not a problem. This equation can be used for prediction within the variable range tested.

TABLE 4—*Correlations of independent variables with each other.*

	Moisture	Fat	Protein	*l*	*a*	*b*	Load	Slope
Moisture	...	−0.60	−0.08	0.69	−0.15	0.20	0.61	0.27
Fat	...	...	0.06	−0.09	0.13	0.31	−0.37	−0.19
Protein	...	...	...	0.05	0.77	0.33	−0.42	−0.18
l	...	...	...	...	0.09	0.79	0.33	0.03
a	...	...	...	...	...	0.49	−0.77	−0.74
b	...	...	...	...	...	...	−0.17	−0.29
Load	...	...	...	...	...	...	...	0.76
Slope	...	...	...	...	...	...	...	...

Table 5 lists equations developed for overall liking, flavor liking, cheese "just right," and salt "just right." Notice that flavor liking, cheese "just right," and salt "just right," are all predicted using Hunter *l, a, b* scores. This is because these three consumer responses are all highly correlated with each other (flavor/cheese = 0.86, flavor/salt = 0.85, cheese/salt = 0.91). The same is true for moisture, *b* and slope predicting overall, and flavor liking (overall/flavor = 0.96). Also notice that no equation is entirely without issue, that is, where all independent variables have less correlation with each other than with the dependent variable, and each term and overall model are highly significant with a high R^2. As variables are added to the equations, it becomes more difficult to satisfy all these criteria. Adapting a less strict view of "significant" for variable inclusion, keeping terms in the model that are more highly correlated with each other than with the dependent variable, and using a borderline significant equation or combining two correlated independent variables into one measure may be necessary to generate a useful equation.

b. Stepwise Regression

The equation using overall liking as the dependent variable was developed using the stepwise procedure, limiting the model to three terms or fewer. Using the default *p* value of 0.15 for entry of a term into the model (and for deletion of a term from the model) results in generation of no multivariable equation. Increasing the *p* value for entry and exit to 0.30 results in the equation:

$$\text{overall liking} = -11.47453775 + 0.65304445(\text{fat}) + 0.17685120(b) + 0.02310039\ (\text{slope})$$

with $R^2 = 0.76$, adj $R^2 = 0.58$ and prob(F) = 0.10; significance of coefficients are 0.13, 0.09, and 0.15.

Compare this with the models generated by all possible subsets (Table 5); clearly the model determined using the stepwise procedure is not as good. Once *b* is in the model, *l* and slope or moisture and slope account for more variation than fat and slope; using the stepwise procedure would have given a less useful equation in this case. Additionally, the correlation between two independent variables (*b*/slope) is higher than that between one of them (slope) and the independent variable (overall liking).

Table 6 lists equations generated using the stepwise procedure for the same consumer responses as those in Table 5; because no multivariate equations were generated with the 0.15 default *p* value, *p* of 0.30 was used instead. Notice that no multivariable equation was generated for flavor liking or salt "just right," and a less useful three-variable equation was generated for cheese "just right" than that found using all subsets regression.

In accordance with the previous discussion on allowing curvature in the model, the stepwise regression procedure was rerun using all analytical variables and their squares as independent variables. Interaction terms were not considered because of the large number of additional variables (28) this would create.

For the dependent variables listed in Table 6, in no case was a reasonable multivariable equation containing a quadratic term generated using the 0.15 or 0.30 entry and exit *p* value criterion (in this case, a multivariable equation had at least three, and at most four, terms, an independent variable, its square and another independent variable; the only multivariable equation that was generated had a very low adjusted R^2 and no significant terms in it).

If a squared term is included in a multivariate equation, it is generally recommended to include the linear counterpart as well.

4. Principal Components Regression

Principal components analysis with varimax rotation was conducted with the eight analytical variables. Table 7 gives the correlations between the analytical variables and the three principal

TABLE 5—*All possible subsets regression models.*

Dependent Variable	Model	Prob(1)[a]	Prob(2)[a]	Prob(3)[a]	Prob(F)	R^2	Adj R^2
*Overall Liking	7.337439 + 0.527684(*b*) − 0.458024(l) + 0.03824(slope)	<0.01	<0.01	<0.01	<0.01	0.97	0.95
***Overall Liking	−1.395965 + 0.275041(*b*) − 0.749462(moisture) + 0.03206(slope)	<0.01	0.03	0.03	0.02	0.88	0.80
*Flavor Liking	19.5988 − 0.4763(l) − 0.5313(*a*) + 0.5253(*b*)	0.16	0.31	<0.01	0.03	0.86	0.76
**Flavor Liking	0.887103 − 0.679101(moisture) + 0.205794(*b*) + 0.025161(slope)	0.08	0.05	0.12	0.12	0.74	0.54
*Cheese Just Right	8.165818 − 0.13537(l) + 0.139967(*b*) − 0.198244(*a*)	<0.01	<0.01	<0.01	<0.01	0.96	0.93
***Cheese Just Right	2.412256 − 0.312596(moisture) − 0.317767(load) + 0.044611(*b*)	0.02	0.03	0.04	0.05	0.83	0.70
*Salt Just Right	8.593174 − 0.152124(l) − 0.159293(*a*) + 0.142435(*b*)	<0.01	<0.01	<0.01	<0.01	0.97	9.95
***Salt Just Right	4.734010 − 0.237757(moisture) − 0.094059(*a*) + 0.048528(*b*)	0.01	0.07	0.03	0.04	0.85	0.74

*Highly correlated independent variables.
**Border line significant equation.
***At least one independent variable is more highly correlated with another independent variable than with the dependent variable.
[a]Probability of the 1st, 2nd, and 3rd coefficients in the equation.

TABLE 6—*Equations generated using stepwise regression.*

Dependent Variable	Model	Prob(1)[a]	Prob(2)[a]	Prob(3)[a]	Prob(F)	R^2	Adj R^2
Overall Liking	11.47453775 + 0.6530445(fat) + 0.17685120(*b*) + 0.02310039(slope)	0.13	0.09	0.15	0.10	0.76	0.58
Flavor Liking	No multivariable equation generated	...	...	...	...	...	...
Cheese Just Right	0.97495180 + 0.20933126(fat) + 0.06598838(*a*)	0.06	0.24	...	0.12	0.5	0.40
Salt Just Right	No multivariable equation generated	0.08	0.05	0.12	0.12	0.74	0.54

[a]Probability of the 1st, 2nd, and 3rd coefficients in the equation.

TABLE 7—*Correlations between analytical variables and principal component factors.*

	Principal Component 1	Principal Component 2	Principal Component 3
Moisture	−0.23	0.55	−0.75
Protein	0.75	0.12	−0.13
Fat	0.05	0.13	0.94
1	−0.06	0.96	−0.20
a	0.98	0.18	0.04
b	0.34	0.89	0.23
Load	−0.82	0.23	−0.42
Slope	−0.75	−0.01	−0.25

components which together account for 86% of the variation. A three-component solution in this case meets the criterion that each component has an eigenvalue greater than 1. After rotation, Principal Component 1 is associated with protein, *a*, load and slope, Principal Component 2 with 1 and *b*, and Principal Component 3 with moisture and fat.

These orthogonal principal components can be used as predictor variables for the consumer responses [*4*]. Because of issues raised in the previous discussion with respect to stepwise regression, all possible subsets regression was used to predict consumer response using the principal components. Table 8 lists the equations developed using varimax rotated principal

TABLE 8—*Regression equations generated using all subsets to predict consumer response from principal components.*

LINEAR TERMS ONLY

	Model	Prob(1)[a]	Prob(2)[a]	Prob(F)	R^2	Adj R^2
Overall Liking	*	...	...	...	...	...
Flavor Liking	*	...	...	...	...	...
Cheese Just Right	3.275 + 0.108496 (Principal Component 3) − 0.0585 (Principal Component 1)	0.20	0.04	0.06	0.69	0.54
Salt Just Right	3.6875 + 0.128463 (Principal Component 3)	<0.01	...	<0.01	0.78	0.74

LINEAR AND QUADRATIC TERMS

	Model	Prob(1)[a]	Prob(2)[a]	Prob(3)[a]	Prob(F)	R^2	Adj R^2
Overall Liking	*	...	...	...	...	...	...
Flavor Liking	5.6425 − 0.3866386 (Principal Component 1) + 0.794619 (Principal Component 3) + 0.622812 (Principal Component 3)^2	0.10	0.02	0.06	0.08	0.79	0.63
Cheese Just Right	3.176875 − 0.12 (Principal Component 1) + 0.186162 (Principal Component 3) + 0.112143 (Principal Component 3)^2	0.04	0.01	0.09	0.04	0.86	0.75
Salt Just Right	**	...	...	...	...	...	...

*Significant equation was not obtained.
**Same model as when only liner terms included.
[a]Probability of the 1st, 2nd, and 3rd coefficients in the equation.

components for the same consumer responses discussed previously. An alternate approach would be to use one variable from each principal component in developing regression equations.

Notice that unlike equations developed using all subsets, significant equations for overall flavor liking were not developed using principal component regression, and the equations developed for cheese and salt "just right" explain less variation than those developed using all subsets regression.

The principal component regressions were rerun using all subsets regression with the three components and their squared terms as independent variables to allow for curvature; three factors and their squared terms yield six variables, the maximum allowed using all subsets regression with only eight observations. Therefore, cross product terms were not included.

Again, a significant equation was not developed for overall liking. Significant equations were developed for flavor liking and cheese "just right" using the same principal component variables; this is logical because the correlation between flavor liking and cheese "just right" is 0.86.

Stepwise regression was also used to generate models using the principal components (3), their squares to allow for curvature (3), and their cross products (3) for a total of nine independent variables. When examining models, a correction was made to always include a linear effect if the cross product or squared term was included in the model. Because of this correction, up to four variables were accepted in the equations.

Table 9 gives models generated using this approach. The equations for overall and flavor liking are quite similar, which is logical as the correlation between these dependent variables is 0.96. A five-variable equation was needed for cheese "just right" and is not included. The equation for salt "just right," is given in Table 8.

IV. Summary

A. The data analysis case study has examined several approaches to understanding relationships between analytical data and consumer response and the use of analytical data to predict consumer response. Recommendations emerging from this discussion are:

1. Always graph relationships prior to data analysis.
2. Consider univariate (linear and quadratic) and multivariate equations for prediction; allow for the possibility of curvature in the models.
3. Be aware of the effects of multicollinearity on the regression equation and interpretation of relationships.
4. Understand limitations when using the stepwise technique compared to all subsets regression.
5. It may be possible to reduce complexity and remove multicollinearity by using principal components as the independent variables in regression; allow for the possibility of curvature in the models.

B. Study

Using all the techniques discussed, the final best understanding of data relationships for selected attributes appears to be:

1. Overall and flavor liking may be predicted by a linear combination of moisture, *b* and slope or by moisture and protein as single variable quadratic functions.

TABLE 9—*Linear, squared, and cross-product terms of the three principal components.*

	Model	Prob(1)[a]	Prob(2)[a]	Prob(3)[a]	Prob(4)[a]	Prob(F)	R^2	Adj R^2
Overall Liking	6.25 − 0.022425 (Principal Component 1) + 0.689378 (Principal Component 3) − 0.575776 (Principal Component 1 × Principal Component 3) + 0.379212 (Principal Component 2)	0.76	<0.01	<0.01	0.01	0.01	0.47	0.92
Flavor Liking	6.1875 − 0.074442 (Principal Component 1) + 0.614886 (Principal Component 3) − 0.458349 (Principal Component 1 × Principal Component 3) + 0.254551 (Principal Component 2)	0.54	0.02	0.05	0.10	0.08	0.89	0.75
Cheese Just Right	*	...	...	...	...	...	...	...
Salt Just Right	**	...	...	...	...	...	...	...

*Five variable model needed.
**Same model as in Table 8.

2. Texture liking may be predicted linearly by fat if an outlier is removed or by moisture as a quadratic function.
3. Color "just right" may be predicted by Hunter *b*.
4. Cheese "just right" may be predicted by a linear combination of moisture, load, and *b*.
5. Salt "just right" may be predicted by a linear combination of moisture, *a*, and *b*.

References

[1] Stevens, J., *Applied Multivariate Statistics for the Social Sciences,* Eribaum, Hillsdale, NJ, 1992.
[2] Draper, N. R. and Smith, H., *Applied Regression Analysis,* Wiley, New York, 1981.
[3] SAS, *SAS/STAT Guide for Personal Computers,* Ver. 6, SAS Institute, Cary, NC, 1987.
[4] Freund, R. J. and Littell, R. C., SAS, *SAS System for Regression,* SAS Institute, Cary, NC, 1986.

by Silvia King[1] *and Judith Heylmun*[2]

Chapter 7—Relationships Between Consumer Acceptance and Consumer/Market Factors

I. Introduction

Sensory consumer tests are usually designed to study the effect of product variables/factors, such as ingredients or processing changes, on consumer acceptance. Conclusions and recommendations are based on the effect of product factors on consumer acceptance. For example, the consumer response may have changed as a result of an ingredient change. If the product is to remain the same, further work on ingredient substitution is recommended based on these results.

On the other hand, the outcome of a consumer study may be influenced by parameters other than those relating to the product, such as consumer/market factors. These may include: gender, age, ethnic background, location or region, product usage patterns, etc. Keeping the test objective in mind, the design of the consumer test should incorporate the study of these consumer factors and their effect on consumer acceptance whenever possible.

There is value in understanding how consumer factors affect results. Consumer factors may or may not lead to changes in the sensory characteristics of the products tested, but consumer factors may influence how a product is marketed. Who will purchase it? Are there gender differences? Does an older segment of the population respond differently than a younger user group? Are there differences between product users based on their location, e.g., East versus West Coast? By understanding these differences, a manufacturer may choose to reformulate a product in order to meet a specific market niche or subgroup. This is commonly referred to as segmentation. Through the use of segmentation, a manufacturer may gain a competitive advantage in the product's positioning that distinguishes it in a meaningful way for the targeted customer. If one location has a greater preference for a specific product, it may be introduced there first. Or the manufacturer may choose to selectively advertise to a specific group of people. For example, if teens demonstrate greater preference for a product, the advertising may be oriented in that direction. By examining consumer/market factors, a company may stop a product introduction, for example, if only a small segment of the population likes the product and marketing the product would not be profitable. On the other hand, a company may market a product that overall looks like a failure but may be a success for a specific market segment.

The purpose of this case study is to demonstrate some of the methods used to relate consumer/market factors with overall consumer acceptance and their value.

[1]Senior sensory analyst, McCormick & Company, Inc., 204 Wight Ave., Hunt Valley, MD 21031.
[2]Director, Analytical Chemistry and Shelf Life, Nabisco, Inc., 200 Deforest Ave., East Hanover, NJ 07936.

II. Approach

A leading food manufacturing company wants to improve one of its key products that has been losing market share over the past few years. The company wants to determine who their current consumers are and how to change the product to regain their former position in the marketplace. As a result, a flavor improvement project was initiated, with several suppliers submitting variations of the key flavor ingredient. It was decided that the submissions would be evaluated using consumer response to determine overall liking of each product. Competitors' products were also included in the sample set for a broader comparison.

Consumer testing was designed:

1. To determine overall consumer acceptability of the current product versus the competition.
2. To identify the best alternative flavor that would result in a product improvement.
3. To determine key consumer/market factors that may influence consumer acceptance and help define a new target population.

A total of 269 respondents participated in the consumer test. Two different locations were selected to administer the test, an East Coast and a West Coast test site. Consumers were pre-selected based on marketing's input. The characteristics are listed in Table 1.

A total of 24 products were selected for evaluation, including the current product, several reformulated versions, and competitor products. The samples were evaluated on three consecutive days, 8 products each day, following a complete block design. The sample presentation was randomized throughout the three days to minimize order effect and day-to-day variation. Each product was rated for overall acceptability based on the product's aroma, flavor, texture, and appearance combined. Overall acceptability was measured on a 9-point hedonic scale, where: 1 = "dislike extremely" . . . to 9 = "like extremely."

Results of the test are presented in Table 2. There were statistically significant differences among the samples. The means for the samples ranged between 5.3 and 6.6. The data were evaluated further to gain a greater understanding of the sample population tested and the relationship between consumer acceptance and consumer factors.

TABLE 1—*Description of consumer/market factors.*

Consumer/Market Factor	Category	No. Respondents/Percent,%
Location	East	133(49)
	West	136(51)
Age	20–24	25(9)
	25–34	87(32)
	35–44	98(36)
	45–54	39(14)
	55–60	20(7)
Gender	Male	36(13)
	Female	233(87)
Product usage patterns	Every day	190(71)
	Once every 2 to 3 days	51(19)
	Once a week	28(10)
Ethnic heritage	African American	71(26)
	White	134(50)
	Hispanic	64(24)

TABLE 2—*Mean acceptance values for each sample.*

Sample	Mean	Sample	Mean
1	5.7	13	5.7
2	5.8	14	5.5
3	5.4	15	6.6
4	5.3	16	6.4
5	6.3	17	5.4
6	5.9	18	5.9
7	6.2	19	5.6
8	5.7	20	5.3
9	6.5	21	6.1
10	5.5	22	6.3
11	6.2	23	6.4
12	6.4	24	6.2

NOTE: Where 1 = "dislike extremely" . . . 9 = "like extremely."

III. Data Analysis

The data analysis and results presented in this chapter relate only to the third objective cited in the approach, that is, to study the effect of consumer/market factors on consumer acceptance of the products.

The following data analyses assume that judges rated the products significantly different in overall acceptability. Although it will not be discussed in detail, results of the general linear model (GLM) procedure indicated that there were statistically significant differences among the samples as well as the judges at the 99% level of confidence.

This paper focuses primarily on the evaluation of interactions. An interaction is "a measure of the extent to which the effect of changing the level of one factor depends on the level(s) of another or others" [*1*].

The data analysis approach [*2–4*] includes the following steps:

A. Assessment of Consumer Factors Two-Way Interactions

Analysis of variance (ANOVA) using a split plot design is used to determine significant interactions. The demographic factors are "nested within" each respondent, indicating that differences between demographic variables are associated with differences between respondents. While the product factor is crossed with each respondent, indicating differences between products is associated with the within judge effect.

Identification of the two sources of error leads to the analysis of the data by a split plot model. A split plot model recognizes that factors applied to main plots (demographic variables) are subjected to larger experimental errors (between respondents) than those applied to subplots (products and within respondent error). Therefore, different variances are used to conduct the proper tests of significance.

The model for this experiment is: gender, age, usage, location, and ethnic group tested by the respondents nested within gender, age, usage, location, and ethnic group factor. This piece is called the whole or the main plot. The remainder of the model or subplot portion consists of the product and the five cross products between demographic variables and product. All terms in the subplot are tested by the residual error.

Results from this analysis will indicate which consumer factors show interactions and need to be further explored.

B. Study of Consumer Factors

ANOVA is used to determine those consumer factors that are significant and do not present Consumer Factor x product interactions. The individual differences among consumer factor categories are studied using tables and frequency distributions.

C. Study of Consumer Factor Interactions

Study of interactions between consumer/market factors is accomplished by plotting two consumer factors at a time and comparing overall acceptability patterns; e.g., age and gender interactions can be evaluated by plotting the mean acceptance values for each age category versus each gender category. These plots are visually inspected for interactions. Note that interaction effects will be limited to a two-level interaction.

IV. Results

A. Assessment of Consumer Factors Two-Way Interactions

The ANOVA results are presented in Table 3. There were significant interactions: Location x product and Ethnic Group x product. Tables 4 and 5 show the product means by location and ethnic group, respectively. These tables have to be assessed to interpret those interactions.

The difference between the overall mean for each location was not statistically significant (6.0 for East Coast versus 5.9 for West Coast). However, the significance of the Location x product interaction suggests the need to compare the location means on a product-by-product basis to understand what may be driving the interaction.

Inspection of Table 4 shows that consumers from the East Coast rated some of the products significantly higher than the West Coast, such as Products 3, 14, and 20. If a greater sample difference existed by location, this information could be used in determining what drives acceptability in one location over the other. If only one-way ANOVA results had been considered, it would have been concluded that there were no differences between products due to location, and possible differences in location would have been missed.

This finding can be used collectively with other results to select the best product. If the product is to be sold nationally, the selection should be based on a product that performed well in both locations. On the other hand, if the sale of the product is going to be location specific, that is, two products will be sold, one in the East Coast and one in the West Coast, this table can help select the products. In this case, Products 15 and 9 received higher scores overall and rated high in both locations; therefore, either of these two products could be selected for a national launch after all other results have been considered.

Table 5 shows results for ethnic heritage. Initial evaluation of the means indicated that there were no differences among the three ethnic groups. ANOVA results suggested an interaction between product and ethnic heritage. Therefore, the differences between ethnic categories are product dependent. Further breakdown of the means on Table 5 indicate that products were liked differently among the categories. African Americans rated Sample 22 highest (6.7), while white and hispanic categories rated Sample 15 highest (6.7). These results reaffirm the importance of evaluating interaction effects before making conclusions about the individual categories. If it were necessary to select one product for all three ethnic backgrounds, one might choose the product with the highest mean in all three ethnic groups.

B. Study of Consumer Factors

Mean differences can be visualized and analyzed using frequency distributions. Frequency distributions are a helpful tool for evaluating judges' use of the scale. Frequency distributions

TABLE 3—*Analysis of variance (split plot model).*

Dependent Variable: OVERALL ACCEPTABILITY

Source	DF	Sum of Squares	Mean Square	*F* Value	*Pr > F*
Model	521	8153.01770	15.64879	4.43	0.0001
Error	5920	20896.70413	3.52985		
Corrected Total	6441	29049.72183			

R-Square	C.V.	Root MSE	OVERALL Mean
0.280657	31.68698	1.87879	5.92921

Source	DF	Type III SS	Mean Square	*F* Value	*Pr > F*
GENDER	1	87.88732	87.88732	24.90	0.0001
AGE	4	147.54319	36.88580	10.45	0.0001
USAGE	2	138.53853	69.26927	19.62	0.0001
LOCATION	1	0.14691	0.14691	0.04	0.8384
ETHNIC	2	49.81836	24.90918	7.06	0.0009
RE*GE*AG*USA*LOC*ETH	258	5558.47690	21.54448	6.10	0.0001
PRODUCT	23	243.95269	10.60664	3.00	0.0001
GENDER*PRODUCT	23	101.37721	4.40770	1.25	0.1904
AGE*PRODUCT	92	308.40972	3.35228	0.95	0.6165
USAGE*PRODUCT	46	211.00771	4.58712	1.30	0.0846
LOCATION*PRODUCT	23	225.89743	9.82163	2.78	0.0001
ETHNIC*PRODUCT	46	317.47116	6.90155	1.96	0.0001

Tests of Hypotheses Using the Type III MS for RE*GE*AG*USA*LOC*ETH as an Error Term

Source	DF	Type III SS	Mean Square	*F* Value	*Pr > F*
GENDER	1	87.887322	87.887322	4.08	0.0444
AGE	4	147.543188	36.885797	1.71	0.1477
USAGE	2	138.538535	69.269267	3.22	0.0418
LOCATION	1	0.146908	0.146908	0.01	0.9343
ETHNIC	2	49.818358	24.909179	1.16	0.3163

also provide an insight on how the different categories for each consumer/market factor differed from each other. Although results of the frequency distributions are reflected in the mean values, it is important to visually inspect the data for abnormalities in the use of the scale, such as bimodal distributions. The consumer/market factors were separated into their respective categories, and frequency distributions for each were evaluated by plotting the overall acceptability percent frequency response versus each consumer/market factor.

Figures 1 and 2 show the skewness of the data towards the upper portion of the scale. This skewness is expected since the judges were pre-selected based on their liking for this type of product.

ANOVA results (Table 3) show that the consumer factors of gender and product usage are significant effects. The individual categories for these factors need to be assessed.

Table 6 shows the mean values for the categories within each of these consumer factors.

Gender differences indicate that males rated the samples higher than females in overall acceptability (6.2 versus 5.9). This is important since females are the target population for this product and 87% of the responses for this test were provided by females.

TABLE 4—*Mean values for each sample by location.*

Sample	Location	
	East	West
1	5.5	6.0
2	5.5	6.0
3[a]	5.9	5.0
4	5.2	5.5
5	6.2	6.3
6	5.9	6.0
7	6.1	6.3
8	5.9	5.5
9	6.7	6.4
10	5.5	5.6
11	6.2	6.2
12	6.4	6.3
13	5.5	5.8
14[a]	6.1	5.0
15	6.8	6.5
16	6.5	6.3
17	5.4	5.4
18	5.9	5.9
19	5.7	5.6
20[a]	5.7	4.9
21	6.1	6.1
22	6.4	6.2
23	6.5	6.3
24	6.0	6.4
Mean	6.0	5.9

NOTE: $LSD_{.05} = 0.5$.
[a]Indicates a statistically significant difference at $a = 0.05$.

Evaluation of the mean values for product usage pattern suggest that daily users of this product (71% of total respondents) rated the acceptability of the products higher than the other two groups.

Once the consumer factors have been selected, overall acceptability responses for the products within each factor can be used to select the most acceptable product.

Overall, Product 15 had the highest score for overall acceptability, followed very closely by Products 9, 23, and 16. These results were driven by females (mean score of 6.6), high product users (6.7) between the ages of 35 to 44 (6.7) and 45 to 54 (6.5). Since this is the current target population, it would be concluded that these products have the highest overall acceptability and will probably be used by the marketing group to select their new launch. In this case, ingredient and production cost may be the limiting factors in selecting one product over the other.

C. Study of Consumer/Market Factor Interactions

Interaction effects between consumer factors were visually evaluated by plotting consumer factors against each other. Plotting interactions provides a fast and simple method to determine the relationship between consumer factors and overall acceptability for the factors, including gender, age, and ethnic background. Interactions provide an indication of the effect of factors (e.g., age) on overall acceptance. Analysis of variance was not used to determine significant interaction effects due to missing cell values.

TABLE 5—*Mean values for each sample by ethnic group.*

Sample	Ethnic		
	African American	White	Hispanic
1	5.9	5.5	6.0
2[a]	6.5	5.5	5.8
3	5.1	5.6	5.5
4[a]	5.9	5.0	5.4
5	6.4	6.2	6.1
6	5.9	5.8	6.3
7	6.3	6.1	6.2
8[a]	5.3	6.0	5.6
9	6.2	6.6	6.7
10[a]	6.0	5.2	5.6
11	5.9	6.3	6.5
12	6.5	6.2	6.4
13	5.6	5.6	5.8
14[a,b]	5.0	5.7	5.7
15	6.3	6.7	6.8
16	6.1	6.4	6.6
17	5.6	5.2	5.6
18	6.0	5.8	6.1
19	6.0	5.4	5.8
20[a]	4.9	5.6	5.1
21[c]	6.3	5.8	6.5
22[a]	6.7	6.0	6.4
23	6.6	6.4	6.2
24	6.2	6.0	6.5
Mean	5.9	5.9	6.0

[a]African American vs White $LSD_{.05} = 0.6$.
[b]African American vs Hispanic $LSD_{.05} = 0.7$.
[c]Hispanic vs White $LSD_{.05} = 0.6$.

Visual inspection of the graphs suggested interactions between all of the factors. Figure 3 shows a case where interactions and non-interactions exist. The lines in this graph represent the user group categories, and the x-axis represents each gender category. In this case, there was an interaction between gender and user group. There was a gender interaction between medium users and the other user groups, while no interaction was found between high and low users.

Another example of interaction effects is presented in Fig. 4. This graph compared gender x ethnic interactions. Although the overall ethnic results were not statistically significant, there were some differences between ethnic categories due to gender effect. Whites rated the samples lower than African Americans or hispanics. However, the interaction plot suggests that not all whites followed this trend. Males rated the products higher than females; however, since females accounted for the majority of the responses, the overall mean was lower. It should be noted, however, that gender results for the other ethnic groups remained virtually identical regardless of gender because gender response differences were specific to the white population only.

The following is a summary of the different factor interactions:

1. Gender Effect—Interaction plots with other consumer factors suggested that gender effects existed in specific subcategories including medium product users (6.4 versus 5.6) presented

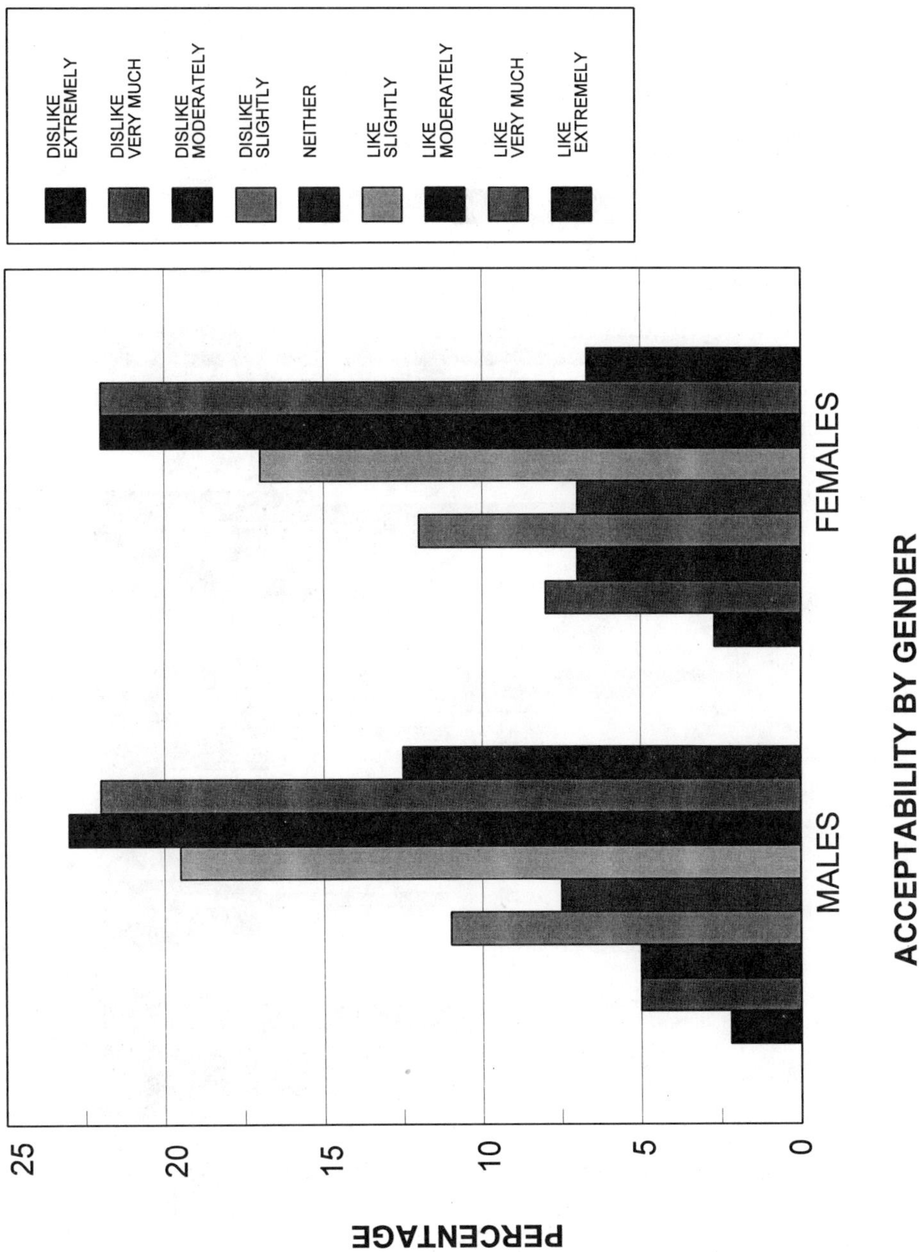

FIG. 1—*Percent response for samples by gender.*

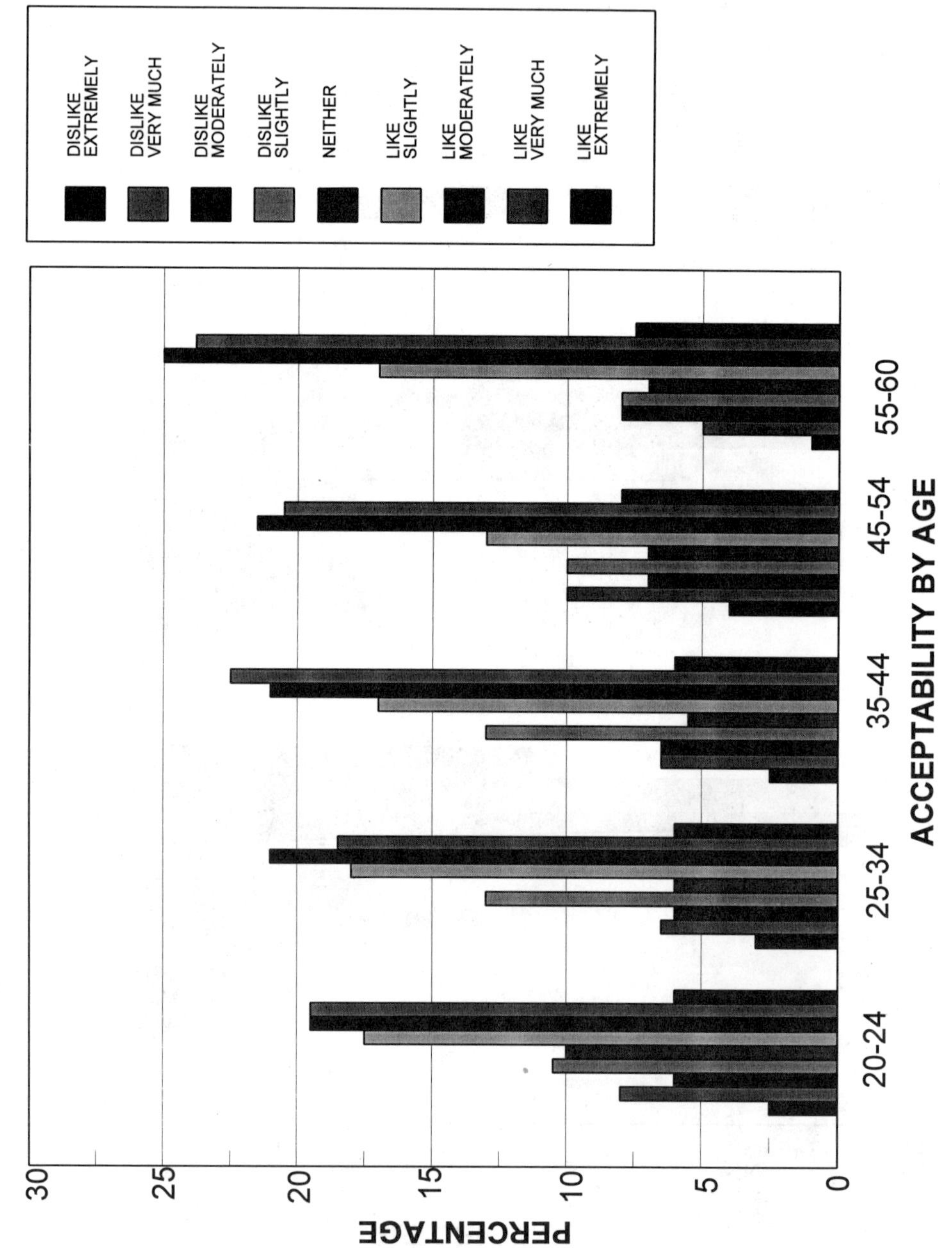

FIG. 2—*Percent response for samples by age group.*

TABLE 6—*Mean values and Duncan's results for each consumer/market factor category.*

Consumer/Market Factors	Category	Mean Value
Location	East	6.0
	West	5.9
Age	20–24	5.8
	25–34	5.9
	35–44	6.0
	45–54	5.8
	55–60	6.3
Gender[a]	Male	6.2a
	Female	5.9b
Product usage patterns[a]	Every day	6.0a
	Once every 2 to 3 days	5.7b
	Once a week	5.7b
Ethnic heritage	African American	6.0
	White	5.9
	Hispanic	6.0

[a]Where age, gender, and product usage were statistically significant at the 95% level of confidence.
a,b = Duncan's test indicating which samples are similar to each other at the 95% level of confidence.

in Fig. 3, 45 to 54 age group (6.9 versus 5.7) and white ethnic group (6.5 versus 5.8) presented in Fig. 4, where males consistently rated the samples higher than females. However, it must be noted that the percent male population in this test was very small; therefore, the impact of these sub-categories on the overall mean is small. Nevertheless, this information can be used to further investigate the possibility of a new target market.

2. Age Effect—The largest effect is observed in the Age x user group interaction, where the 45 to 54 age group rated products differently based on their use of the product. High users within this age category rated the products higher (6.5) than medium users (4.5), suggesting this age group may be the primary target.

3. User Group Effect—There were User Group x gender and User Group x age interactions that were already discussed. Overall, heavy users rated the products higher than medium or low users. This trend remained consistent throughout most of the interaction evaluations. Figure 5 is an exception to this conclusion. This graph compares User Group x ethnic group interaction effects. The high user group effect was only specific to the white population. African American scores remained consistent for all the user groups, while hispanics scores increased with decreased product usage.

All these observations can be used to identify the target population for this product and make recommendations as needed. The technique just described can also be used to identify market segments to be avoided for this type of product by evaluating low rather than high score values.

V. Conclusions

The results of these analyzes can be summarized as follows:

1. There were Factor x product interactions within Location x product and Ethnic Group x product. This result helps reduce the number of factors evaluated in these analyses.

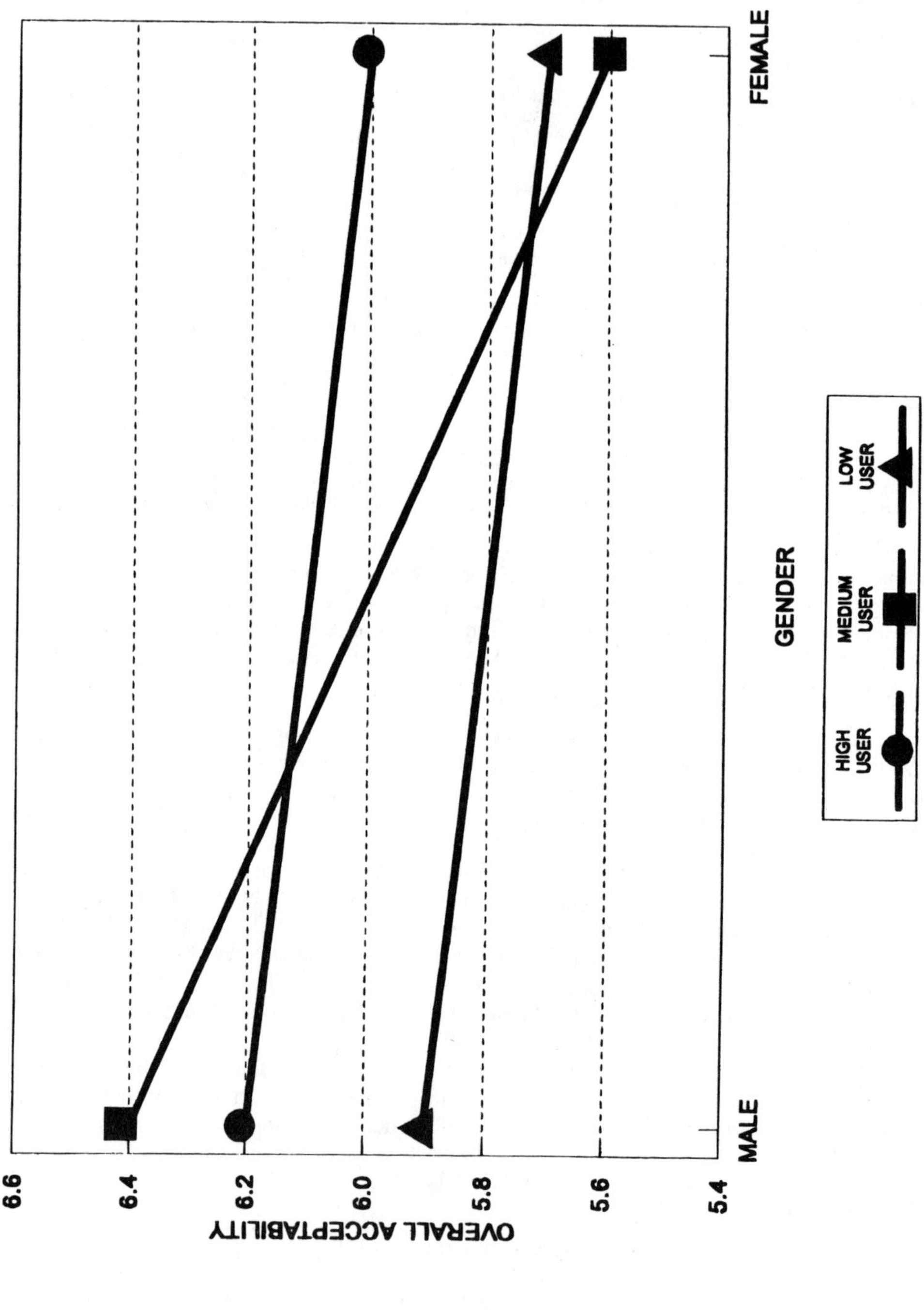

FIG. 3—*Interaction plot for gender versus user group.*

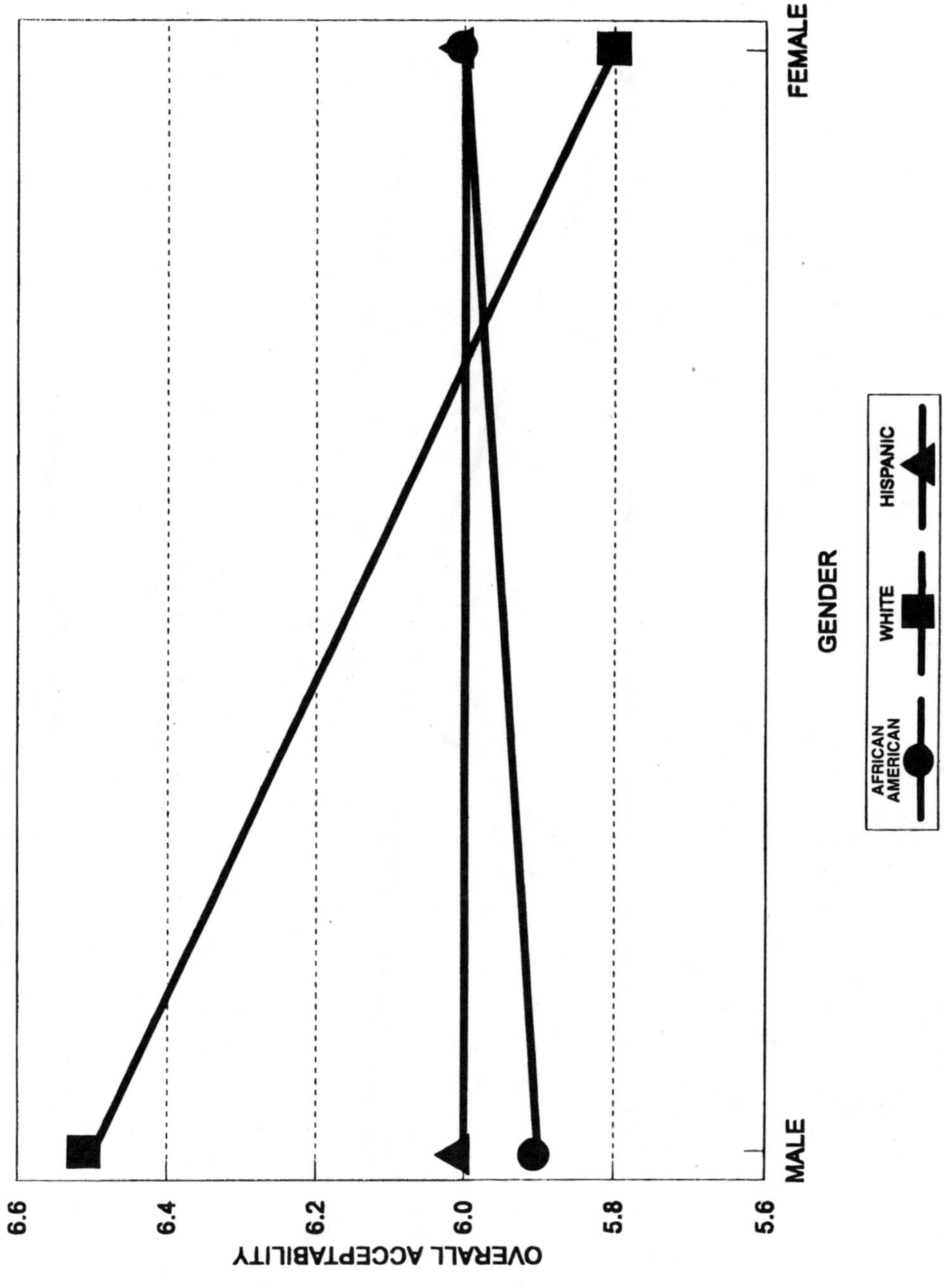

FIG. 4—*Interaction plot for gender versus ethnic group.*

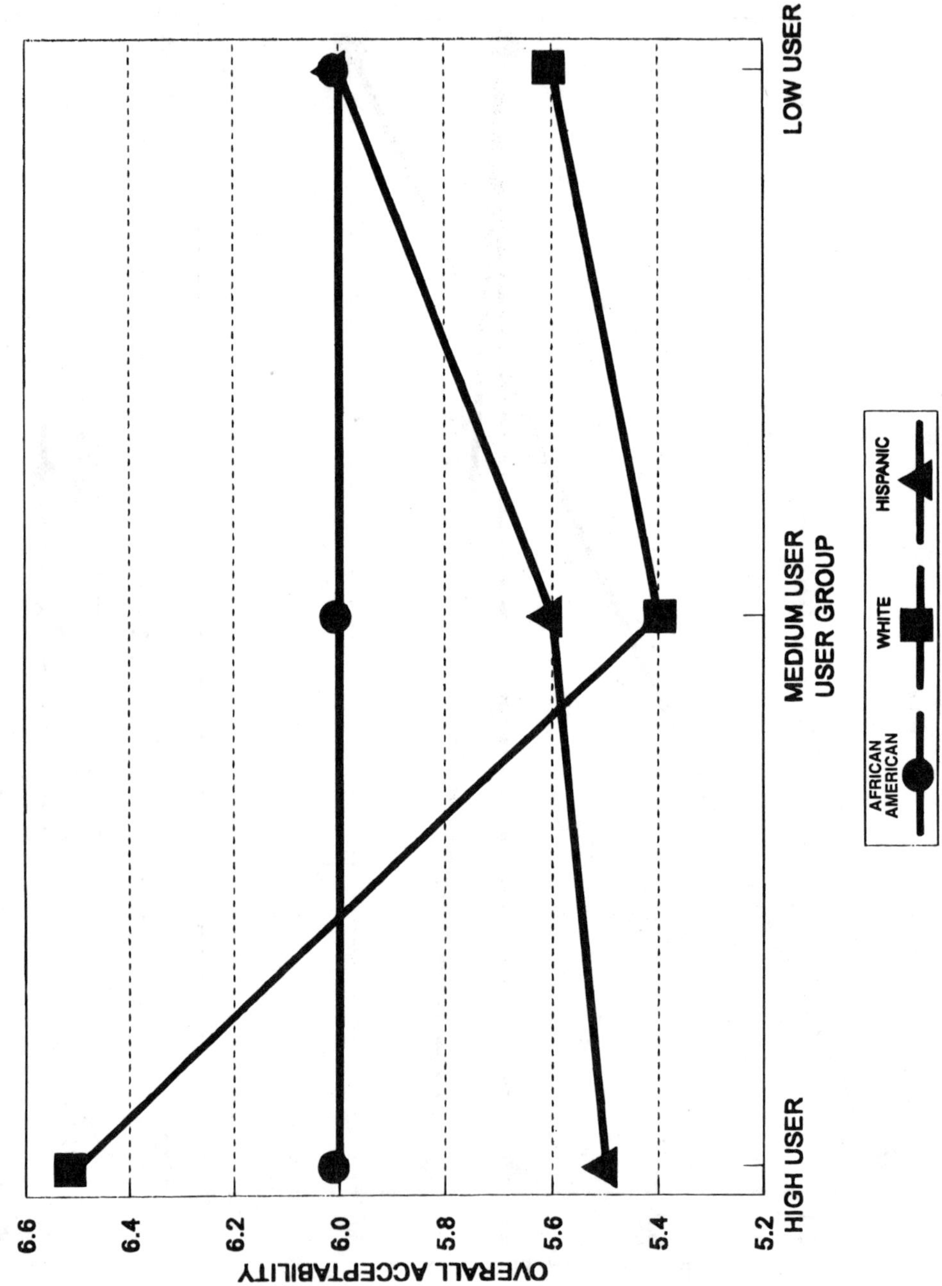

FIG. 5—*Interaction plot for ethnic group versus user group.*

2. It was also concluded that females, heavy users between the ages of 35 and 54, had the greatest impact in the overall results of this test. These categories account for over half of the population tested in this consumer test. Note that the previous comment describes the current target population for this product.
3. Consumer factor interactions uncovered some interesting information about other niches of the population where the product may have new opportunities for growth. These opportunities may be found within the male population, assuming that additional testing is performed to confirm these results and is more focused on the 45 to 54 age range.

This case study demonstrated the value of studying consumer factors and their relationship with consumer acceptance to identify consumer segments and the best target population for a product. The study of consumer factor interactions should be limited to those factors directly related to the objectives of the study. As the number of factors increase within a study, the greater the likelihood of finding a significant interaction due to chance alone.

Acknowledgments

We would like to thank Jason Sapp, senior statistician, Nabisco, Inc., for the comprehensive data analysis and graphs. We would also like to thank Alejandra Muñoz for her suggestions during the preparation of the manuscript.

References

[*1*] Amerine, M. A., Pangborn, R. M., and Roessler, E. B., *Principles of Sensory Evaluation of Food,* Academic Press, New York, 1965, p. 552.
[*2*] Montgomery, D. C., *Design and Analysis of Experiments,* John Wiley & Sons, New York, 1984.
[*3*] Milliken, G. A. and Johnson, D. E., *Analysis of Messy Data Vol. I: Designed Experiments,* Lifetime Learning Publications, 1984.
[*4*] Hicks, C. R., *Fundamental Concepts in the Design of Experiments,* Holt, Rinehart and Winston, 1973.

by Ellen R. Daw[1]

Chapter 8—Relationship Between Consumer and Employee Responses in Research Guidance Acceptance Tests

I. Introduction

From a practical standpoint, it is often desirable for a consumer products company to be able to conduct preliminary acceptance testing with an in-house panel made up of company employees. While results from this type of panel should never be used as a basis for final consumer product decisions, they are useful in the early stages of the product development cycle to predict which formulations are most likely to be successful in further testing or to predict consumer responses to such issues as shelf life expiration based on acceptance. Before these panels can be used with confidence, however, it is necessary to establish an understanding of the true predictive nature of in-house panels when compared to actual consumer responses for the product category of interest.

The techniques and methodologies described here would also be applicable to any situation where it is desirable to compare test results from two separate groups, each supplying hedonic or acceptance measurements. For example, this same basic procedure could be used to compare data from different regions of the country, to compare different age, ethnic, or other demographic groups, or to compare employee acceptance data from different production locations, etc. For additional discussion and background on comparing employee and consumer panels, see Amerine et al. [*1*], Stone and Sidel [*2*], and Mielgaard et al. [*3*].

II. Problem

A food company wanted to determine if their employee panel could be counted on to predict consumer responses to a particular product line that had been selected for improvement reformulation. The line of snacks consisted of three different flavors, an Original and two subsequent line extensions, Ranch and Nacho/Salsa flavors. It would save considerable effort and expense if an in-house employee panel could be used to reliably supply preliminary sensory acceptance data during the various steps in the reformulation process.

III. Objectives

1. Explore the relationships between local-area naive consumer ratings and those of an experienced in-house employee acceptance panel. (While the employee panel was not trained, they were considered experienced due to increased exposure to the products tested.)

[1]Manager, Sensory Evaluation Services, c/o 850 West Street, Wadsworth, OH 44281.

2. Determine if the employee panel could be counted on to reasonably predict the acceptance response of naive consumers to the products tested.

IV. Approach

The three products were tested in a CLT (central location test) format, using the same scorecard and a balanced, monadic sequential serving order with both groups. The in-house panel consisted of non-technical employees, and the consumer group was recruited through a local church. Each group included 112 respondents, 50% men and 50% women, ages 20 to 55, who liked the product category and flavors being tested. The scorecard consisted of four 9-point hedonic scales: overall, flavor, saltiness, and texture acceptance. The products tested were plant produced, of similar age, and each was representative of typical plant production for that item.

V. Data Analysis

A. Theory

Data analysis for a simple study such as this one should be straightforward, following a logical progression that allows for examination of results from each individual group of subjects. This analysis began with a graphical presentation of results, followed by comparisons of the ways in which the different groups of subjects responded to the same products. All these steps led the researcher to be able to make a decision to accept or reject the null hypothesis: "There are no differences in the ways employees or consumers will respond to these products and flavors."

B. Data Analysis Steps

1. Graphical Presentation

Graphical presentation of the data was a critical step in this analysis effort, including attribute and product means, and frequency distribution histograms, which formed the foundation of understanding the different response patterns of the two groups.

2. Analysis of Variance

Analysis of variance techniques were applied. A treatments-by-subjects analysis on each group data set, consumer or employee, gave a preliminary understanding of how the groups responded to the products. After testing for both groups was complete, a split-plot analysis of variance, using products and panel groups as main effects, allowed for exploration of the potential interaction effect between the two panels.

3. Means Separation

Duncan's multiple range test provided means separation, reporting significance at an alpha level of $p <= 0.05$, or a 95% confidence level.

4. Alternative Approach—Chi-Square

An alternative view of response patterns between the groups was achieved by collapsing the numerical scores into categories of negative, neutral, and positive scores and applying the chi-square statistic to the resulting categorical responses. It is included here to point to steps that should be taken when working with different groups of subjects and data that is *truly* categorical in nature.

VI. Results

A. Analysis of Variance—Treatments by Subjects

A treatments-by-subjects analysis of variance was conducted on each group as the individual test cells were completed, with products and judges as main effects. Mean scores from these analyses are shown in Table 1. The data reveal similarities in the way each group ranked the three products, from most to least liked, on each attribute. If the project objective had been to select one of the three alternative flavors for further testing, both panel groups would point to the same general conclusion, i.e., chose the Original flavor, the best-liked product. However, since the stated objective is to explore the relationship between sensory test information from two different sources to determine if the pattern and nature of those responses is similar, a simple examination of the mean scores indicates that additional analysis is required.

B. Means Separation

The mean scores from the employee panel are consistently lower than those from the consumer guidance group, and the patterns of means separation (illustrated by the brackets from the Duncan's test) are different for all attributes between the two groups (see Table 1).

C. Split-Plot Analysis of Variance

The split-plot analysis of variance for which this study was designed, with products as the within variable and panel group (employee or consumer) as the between variable, indicates

TABLE 1—*Summary of hedonic mean scores*[a,b] *by panel group.*

Employee Guidance Panel, n = 112		Consumer Guidance Panel, n = 112	
Overall		Overall	
Original	7.12	Original	7.58
Ranch	6.00	Ranch	7.05
Nacho/Salsa	5.62	Nacho/Salsa	6.77
Flavor		Flavor	
Original	6.79	Original	7.26
Ranch	5.57	Ranch	7.04
Nacho/Salsa	5.20	Nacho/Salsa	6.80
Saltiness		Saltiness	
Original	6.69	Original	7.25
Ranch	5.82	Ranch	7.05
Nacho/Salsa	5.61	Nacho/Salsa	6.68
Texture		Texture	
Original	7.02	Original	7.62
Ranch	6.38	Ranch	7.09
Nacho/Salsa	6.04	Nacho/Salsa	6.73

[a]Mean scores within solid brackets are not significantly different at a 95% confidence level ($p <= 0.05$).
[b]Means within dashed brackets represent interpreted trends based on ranks and individual respondent data at a 90% confidence level ($p <= 0.10$).

ERRATUM FOR MANUAL 30

Table 1 of Chapter 8 by Ellen R. Daw was incorrectly printed.
The corrected table, shown below, replaces the table on page 94 of the book

TABLE 1—*Summary of hedonic mean scores[a,b] by panel group.*

Employee Guidance Panel, $n = 112$		Consumer Guidance Panel, $n = 112$	
Overall		Overall	
Original	7.12	Original	7.58
Ranch	6.00	Ranch	7.05
Nacho/Salsa	5.62	Nacho/Salsa	6.77
Flavor		Flavor	
Original	6.79	Original	7.26
Ranch	5.57	Ranch	7.04
Nacho/Salsa	5.20	Nacho/Salsa	6.80
Saltiness		Saltiness	
Original	6.69	Original	7.25
Ranch	5.82	Ranch	7.05
Nacho/Salsa	5.61	Nacho/Salsa	6.68
Texture		Texture	
Original	7.02	Original	7.62
Ranch	6.38	Ranch	7.09
Nacho/Salsa	6.04	Nacho/Salsa	6.73

[a]Mean scores within solid brackets are not significantly different at a 95% confidence level ($p <= 0.05$).
[b]Means within dashed brackets represent interpreted trends based on ranks and individual respondent data at a 90% confidence level ($p <= 0.10$).

significant product and panel differences on all attributes. Most important are the product-by-panel interactions, which are highly significant (>99% confidence) for overall and flavor, with a trend toward significant product-by-panel interaction for saltiness (>90% confidence). Product-by-panel interactions are not significant for texture ratings. SAS (Statistical Analysis Software)®[2] output from the split-plot Anova for flavor and texture is included in Table 2.

D. Graphical Presentations

Figures 1 and 2 show plots of the mean scores for all three products on all four attributes and illustrate differences in how each panel responded to the products. Employee mean scores were lower than consumer scores, which might well be expected. However, the different *pattern* of responses, particularly for the Nacho/Salsa and Ranch products, points the way towards understanding the product by panel interactions. Figure 3 displays the pattern of interaction for flavor scores, as contrasted with texture, shown in Fig. 4, where no interaction occurred. To better understand these different response patterns, histogram plots were prepared of all the distributions of hedonic scores for each product and attribute.

TABLE 2—*Analysis of variance tables—flavor and texture attributes.*

SAS ANOVA OUTPUT—FLAVOR

Tests of Hypotheses using the Anova MS for JUDGE(PANEL) as an error term.

Source	DF	Anova SS	Mean Square	*F* Value	*Pr* > *F*
PANEL	1	236.9063	236.9063	51.39	0.0001

Tests of Hypotheses using the ANOVA MS for JUDGE*PROD(PANEL) as an error term.

Source	DF	Anova SS	Mean Square	*F* Value	*Pr* > *F*
PROD	2	123.4911	61.7455	24.73	0.0001
PROD*PANEL	2	42.2946	21.6473	8.67	0.0002

SAS ANOVA OUTPUT—TEXTURE

Tests of Hypotheses using the Anova MS for JUDGE(PANEL) as an error term.

Source	DF	Anova SS	Mean Square	*F* Value	*Pr* > *F*
PANEL	1	76.006	76.006	20.6	0.0001

Tests of Hypotheses using the ANOVA MS for JUDGE*PROD(PANEL) as an error term.

Source	DF	Anova SS	Mean Square	*F* Value	*Pr* > *F*
PROD	2	100.6071	50.3036	28.62	0.0001
PROD*PANEL	2	0.369	0.1845	0.1	0.9004

[2]SAS Institute, Inc., SAS Campus Drive, Cary, NC 27513.

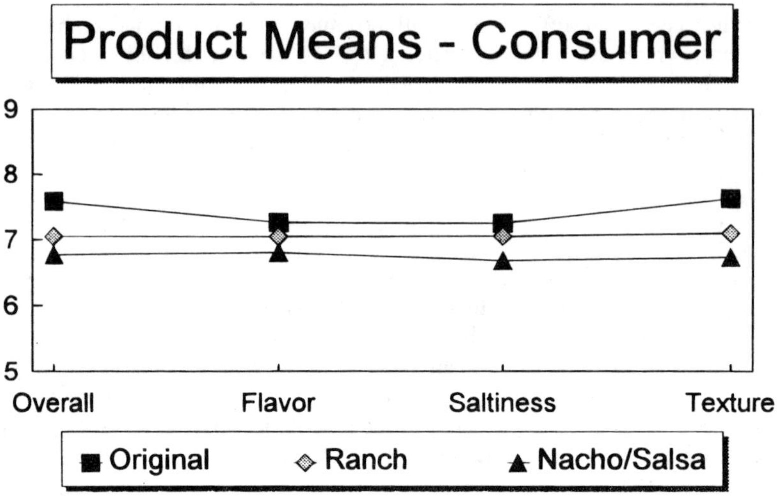

FIG. 1—*Consumer acceptance mean scores for all products.*

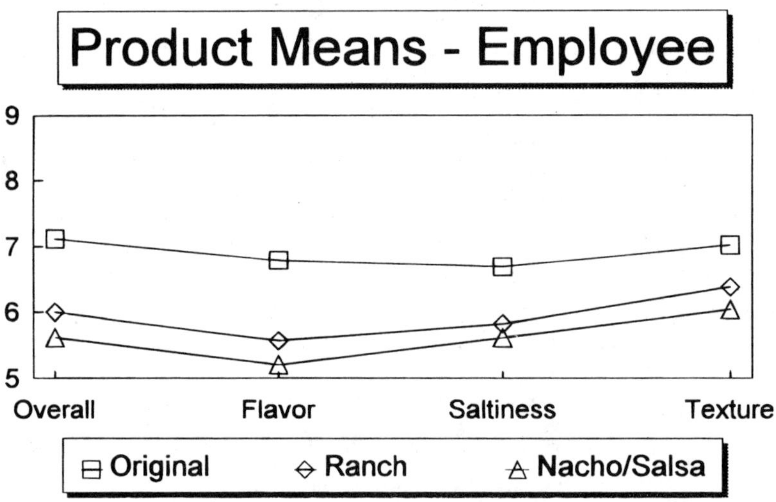

FIG. 2—*Employee acceptance mean scores for all products.*

E. Frequency Histograms

Figure 5 is a graph of the scoring distributions for flavor, from both panels, for the Nacho/Salsa product and is one illustration of the nature of the product-by-panel interaction. There is a bimodal scoring pattern to the employee panel results, with a large negative response to the product. This bimodal pattern was evident in employee responses to both the Ranch and the Nacho/Salsa products on attributes of overall liking, flavor, and saltiness. Such a response pattern was not apparent in consumer responses to any of the three products, nor in employee responses to the Original variety.

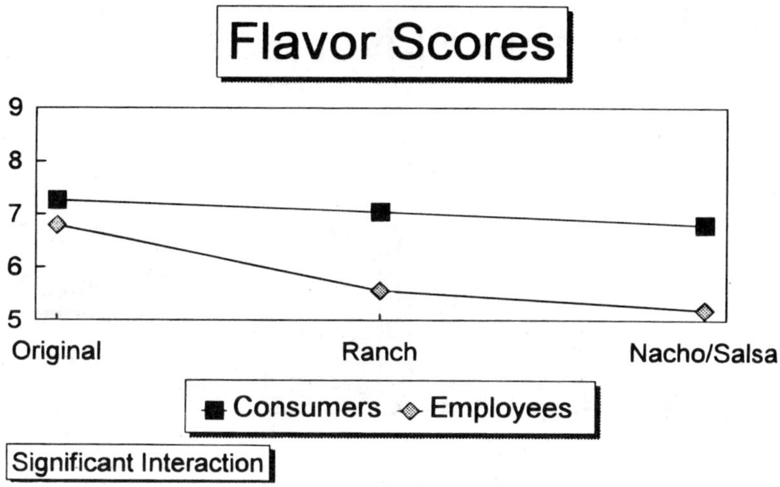

FIG. 3—*Consumer and employee flavor scores showing product-by-panel interactions.*

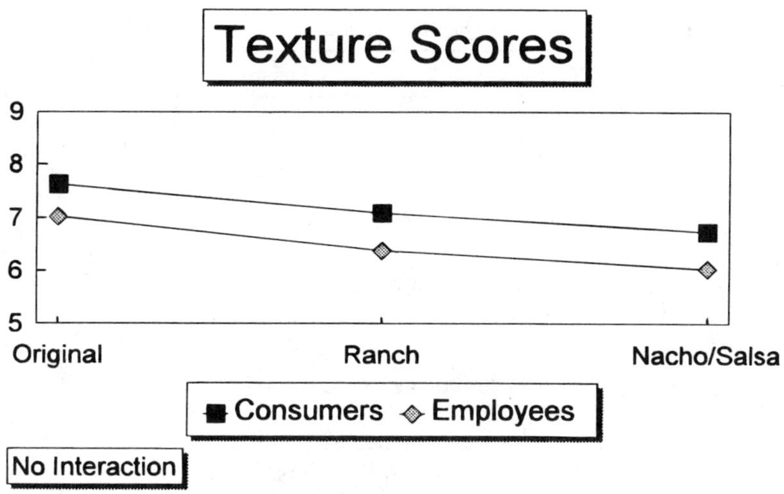

FIG. 4—*Consumer and employee texture scores with no interaction evident.*

F. An Alternative Approach—Chi Square

By collapsing the numeric hedonic scores into categories representing negative ratings (dislike extremely to dislike moderately, 1 to 3), neutral ratings (dislike slightly to like slightly, 4 to 6), and positive ratings (like moderately to like extremely, 7 to 9), it is possible to apply the chi-square statistic to the categorized data as an additional means of comparing the pattern of responses from the two groups. Outcome from the SAS chi-square analysis of flavor scores for the Nacho/Salsa product is shown in Table 3. Employees tended to be more negative and neutral and less positive than the consumers. In total, the chi-square analysis confirmed significant differences between the response patterns of the two panel groups to both the Nacho/Salsa and Ranch products on all attributes.

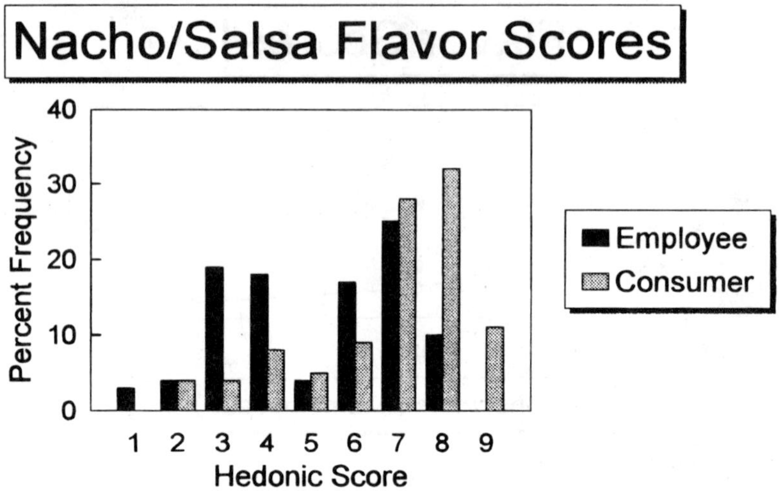

FIG. 5—*Distribution of Nacho/Salsa flavor scores showing bimodal distribution in employee panel.*

TABLE 3—*Categorized flavor scores for Nacho/Salsa—chi-square comparisons by panel.*

	Consumer	Employee	Total
Negative (1–3)			
Frequency	8	29	37
Expected	18.5	18.5	
Neutral (4–6)			
Frequency	24	43	67
Expected	33.5	33.5	
Positive (7–9)			
Frequency	80	40	120
Expected	60	60	
Total	112	112	224

STATISTIC FOR TABLE OF FLAVOR BY PANEL, NACHO/SALSA PRODUCT

Statistic	DF	Value	Prob
Chi-square	2	30.64	0.000

VII. Summary

The results of this preliminary study indicated significant differences in the way employees and consumers responded to these three products. Employees consistently rated the products lower than did the consumer group. While both panels responded similarly to the Original flavor product, employees and consumers responded very differently to the Nacho/Salsa and Ranch products. The employee panel exhibited a far more negative response to the Nacho/Salsa and Ranch products on three of the four attributes than did the consumer group. Given the significant product-by-panel interactions evident in this data set and the significant differences in response patterns between the two panels, it would not be possible to reliably predict the acceptance responses of consumers to Nacho/Salsa and Ranch reformulation efforts using employee panel ratings. Actual consumer guidance testing should be the approach used for preliminary decision making during this reformulation project.

This case study shows the importance of comparing the responses of company employees to those of naive consumers in order to assess the risks associated with the use of *only* employee panels for sensory evaluation purposes. In many cases, employee responses are predictive of consumer responses, and the practice of using employees offers time and cost savings advantages. Studies such as these allow for a relatively quick assessment of the risks involved in using employees to predict consumer responses for a specific type of product and lend confidence to decisions regarding future use of employee panels for particular product assessments.

References

[1] Amerine, M. A., Pangborn, R. M., and Roessler, E. B., *Principles of Sensory Evaluation of Food,* Academic Press, Inc., New York, 1965.

[2] Stone, H. and Sidel, J. L., *Sensory Evaluation Practices,* 2nd ed., Academic Press, Inc., New York, 1993.

[3] Meilgaard, M., Civille, G. V., and Carr, B. T., *Sensory Evaluation Techniques,* CRC Press, Inc., Boca Raton, FL, 1987.

Subject Index